NOTARY PUBLIC

PRACTICES
&
GLOSSARY

About the Author
Founder of the National Notary Association, Raymond C. Rothman has, for over 25 years, dealt extensively with Notaries and notarial practice. He is an internationally respected authority and consultant and has traveled widely in an attempt to bridge the professional gap between American Notaries and their foreign counterparts. His first Notary book was translated into Japanese. Mr. Rothman is a graduate of the School of Business Administration, University of California at Los Angeles.

NOTARY PUBLIC

Practices
&
Glossary

RAYMOND C. ROTHMAN

Since 1957

NATIONAL NOTARY ASSOCIATION
Woodland Hills, California

Library of Congress Cataloging in Publication Data

Rothman, Raymond C.   1922 -
    Notary public practices & glossary.

    Includes index and six appendices.
    1. Notaries — United States. I. Title.
KF8797.R69   347′.73′16   77-93911
ISBN 0-933134-03-7

Library of Congress Catalog No. 77-93911

Printed in the United States of America

Third Printing

Acknowledgments

My sincere appreciation and thanks to the editors of *The National Notary* magazine and publications staff of the National Notary Association. My continuing gratitude is extended to Eleanor Towles-Gernert, who edited my first Notary book in 1966, thus making the writing of this book so much easier.

R.C.R.

PREFACE

It has been my good fortune to serve the State of California as governor for eight years and as an attorney for over fifty years. In these many years of private and public service, I have on numerous occasions required the assistance of Notaries Public.

From my experience I have found Notaries to be conscientious and intelligent public officers with a great respect for the importance of their public obligations. All too often, however, this sense of responsibility has been thwarted by a lack of good information on the proper performance of notarial acts.

Mr. Rothman's book has filled this void in Notary information. With *Notary Public Practices & Glossary,* the conscientious Notary finds an invaluable guide on proper Notary practices and procedures. In clear, nontechnical language all aspects of notarial work are explained from the taking of acknowledgments to voter absentee ballot procedures to a complete glossary of Notary terms and practices.

In addition to making the Notary conscious of his responsibilities and obligations, the book also informs him of the limitations and liabilities of his practices. To faithfully serve the public, the Notary must be aware of these situations in which he is not qualified to act so that he does not do his constituents and himself a disservice.

Clearly, an immeasurable service has been rendered to Notaries, attorneys and the public with the publication of this book. I expect it will soon become a mandatory and much used text in every law library and many governmental agencies throughout the United States.

Fundamental to the workings of our society is the recognition by elected and appointed public officers of the great public trust invested in them in the performance of their duties. *Notary Public Practices & Glossary* will provide Notaries with the essential tools and information needed to perform their notarial obligations with full regard to this enormous trust and responsibility. I can only add that it has increased my respect for and understanding of the American Notary Public.

Edmund G. Brown
Governor of California
1958-1967

CONTENTS

Preface   vi
Introduction   xii
PART I   NOTARY PUBLIC PRACTICES

Chapter 1   HISTORY   1
  Roman Times   1
  The Notary in the United States   2
  Early Responsibilities and Powers   3
  Enactment of Notary Laws   6
  Questions   7

Chapter 2   THE NEED FOR NOTARIAL ACTS   9
  What is A Notary Public?   9
  Questions   10

Chapter 3   THE IMPORTANCE OF
NOTARIZATION   11
  Notarization Defined   11
  Why Notarization is Necessary   11
  Photocopying Machines and Seal Embossers   12
  Questions   13

Chapter 4   POWERS AND FUNCTIONS   15
  Acknowledgment Defined   15
  The Acknowledgment Certificate   16
  Identifying the Signer   17
  Acknowledgment is Made Freely and Voluntarily   19
  Proofs of Acknowledgment   20
  Signature By Mark   21
  Absentee Voter's Ballot   21

Oaths, Affirmations, and Affidavits   23
Certified Copies   25
Negotiable Instruments and Depositions   27
Questions   27

Chapter 5   PROCEDURES   29
Official Signature and Testimonium Clause   29
Official Seal Embosser   30
Photocopying Machines and Forgery   31
How and Where to Use the Seal Embosser   32
Rubber Stamp Seal   34
Record Book of Official Acts (Journal)   35
Entries in the Record Book (Journal)   36
Summary of Practices   42
Questions   43

Chapter 6   LIMITATIONS AND OBLIGATIONS   45
The Practice of Law   45
Mental and Physical Qualifications   46
The Recorder of Public Documents   47
Competence of the Parties   48
Certificate of Authority   49
Disqualifying Interest   51
Questions   52

Chapter 7   CIVIL AND CRIMINAL LIABILITY   53
Civil Liability   53
The Notary Public Bond   54
Criminal Liability   55
Notary Errors and Omissions Insurance   56
Questions   56

Chapter 8   20TH CENTURY NOTARIAL ACTS   59
Computer Signatures and Photocopiers   59
Combating Forgery   60
Questions   62

PART II   NOTARY PUBLIC GLOSSARY   67

APPENDICES   113
Introduction to Appendix   115
Appendix A
  Draft Legislation and Commentary for a
  Uniform Notary Act   119
Appendix B
  Rules of Notarial Practice   161
Appendix C
  Associations Whose Members Are Often
  Notaries Public   167
Appendix D
  Officers in Each State Who Appoint
  Notaries Public   171
Appendix E
  National Notary Census   179
Appendix F
  Sample Forms for Certificates of
  Acknowledgment and Certified Copy   183

INDEX   189

INTRODUCTION

This book is addressed to attorneys, accountants, real estate brokers and agents, court reporters, banking and securities personnel, insurance agents and brokers and all others who have need for the services of a Notary Public. Until the late 1800's a Notary Public served as Recorder of Documents and legal advisor because there were few attorneys available in a population that was thinly scattered over the United States. A hundred years ago the average person had little if any need for a Notary Public because dealings in real property were rare and many people did not even have the opportunity to learn to read and write.

During the last one-hundred years, we have seen the invention of the typewriter, machine photocopying and the ability to store and recover records with the aid of a computer and microscopic reduction of records in a matter of a few seconds. The advances made in transportation and communication all point to even more phenomenal developments in the future. What, then, is the role of the Notary Public in this age of rapidly changing and expanding technology? Is he still needed? If so, what is he needed for? How should he effectively perform his notarization? What is a notarization? Are the Notary customs and Notary laws adopted many years ago still applicable today in the light of the advances made in photocopying? The author has attempted to answer these questions in order to enable today's Notary Public to perform his function effectively.

It is hoped that this publication will, in addition to its immediate value to every Notary, bring a clearer understanding to all readers of the problems faced by the Notary: Fully cognizant of his liability, both civil and criminal, in connection with the performance of his notarial acts, the Notary is obligated to (1) comply with the statutes in his own state; (2) comply with the statutes in another state, the federal government, or a foreign government; (3) perform his official notarial acts so as to satisfy the desires and expectations of the party who is asking to have his signature notarized, as well as the person or office who is subsequently to rely on the notarization as being a valid and authentic act; and (4) effectively perform his notarial act so that it accomplishes the purposes for which it was intended.

Raymond C. Rothman

Woodland Hills, California
January 1, 1978

Rutherford B. Hayes,

President of the United States of America
To all who shall see these Presents, Greeting:

Know Ye, That, reposing special trust and confidence

do appoint him to be Notary Public for the District of

fulfill the duties of that Office according to Law, and

privileges, and emoluments thereunto of right appertaining

of five years from the date hereof.

In testimony whereof, I have caused these Letters

hereunto affixed.

Given under my hand, at the City of Washington, the 6th

Lord one thousand eight hundred and *seventy-eight*

of America the 103rd.

By the President:

F. W. Se

r the *Integrity* and *Ability* of *Milton C. Barnard*, I

olumbia; and do authorize and empower him to execute and

to have and to hold the said *Office*, with all the powers,

to him, the said *Milton C. Barnard* —, for the term

be made *Patent* and the seal of the *United States* to be

day of *August* —, in the year of our

and of the *Independence* of the *United States*

R. B. Hayes

cccc(

Acting Secretary of State.

This notarial appointment signed by Rutherford B. Hayes in 1878 and bearing the embossed impression of the Presidential seal characterizes the significance of the notarial office 100 years ago. Milton C. Barnard received three appointments from Presidents Hayes, Cleveland and Harrison.

PART I
NOTARY PUBLIC
PRACTICES

Notaries Public perform a significant service for the conduct of public and private business in this country. Even as the responsibilities of the Notary have increased, so has the professionalism of those who are qualified to affix the seal. As our society becomes increasingly more complex, we can anticipate a growing need for the services of Notaries Public.

GEORGE McGOVERN
U.S. Senator, South Dakota

The work of Notaries Public continues to be an important part in maintaining the integrity of our legalistic society.

ROBERT P. GRIFFIN
U.S. Senator, Michigan

In these days of complex rules and regulations, it is important that many documents be notarized and it is equally important that Notaries Public have a full understanding of the responsibilities of their office.

RUSSELL W. PETERSON
Governor, Delaware

Notaries Public provide an important, but too often unacknowledged public service.

FRANCIS W. SARGENT
Governor, Massachusetts

CHAPTER 1

History

Roman Times

During the Roman period the art of writing was not widespread. It became the duty of a public official, called a Notarius, to put documents in writing and to hold them in safekeeping. These consisted of agreements that persons desired to be made a public record, or agreements and wills that were to be kept in full force and effect.

If the parties to an agreement were not able to write, they used a metal or clay disk, called a "private seal," on which was engraved a distinctive design or coat of arms which served as a signature to the agreement. A sticky wax was melted onto the paper at the end of the document, and the private seal was impressed into the wax.

In the centuries to follow, not only did more people learn to write, but the mechanization of the art of making paper increased its supply. As agreements extended in length to often more than one page, it was customary to make two holes in the margin through the several pages of the agreement and tie the pages together with a ribbon. To make sure that the ribbon would not be broken in order to add or eliminate pages, the Notary melted wax over the knot and impressed it with his official seal. From this Notary's act comes today's definition of the verb "seal," which means to "make secure" or "enclose" an object.

The increase in people reading and writing made it necessary to enact rules and laws to govern the form of agreements. As the work of drawing up laws, contracts, and wills became more complicated, duties that had once been performed by Notaries Public were taken over by attorneys. What was left to the Notary were functions of a nonlegal (ministerial) nature, as they are today. He testified in writing to the identity of the persons who signed and/or affixed their private seal to the agreement; he witnessed the signing of the agreement and took the acknowledgment of the parties that they desired the agreement to be in effect; he took all necessary precautions to ensure that the agreement was properly sealed (in the sense of "made secure") so that it could not be tampered with at a later date by any of the parties to the agreement or another party; and he often was responsible for keeping and preserving the original and only document in a safe place.

The Notary in the United States

In the United States, the colonists had little use for the services of a Notary Public. Their activities and interests were directed toward developing a raw and abundantly endowed land continent, and not toward reading and writing. Most agreements for the purchase and sale of land were made public in open court. The buyer and seller met before an official, such as a judge, to advise him of their intention to make an agreement. The judge would make the agreement official and in full force and effect simply by recording the terms in his court record. During the colonial period Notaries Public were elected or appointed in the same way as judges in each colony. However, their duties were of a ministerial rather than a judicial nature.

The increase in trade between the Colonies and Europe pointed out the need for an official of high moral character, such as the Notary Public, who could witness, as well as draw up, simple agreements for the purchase and sale of merchandise. Colonists used a bill of exchange to pay for merchandise received from Europe and gave it either to the captain of the ship or to another colonist who had sold merchandise to the business house in Europe. Thus, the bill of exchange was a kind of check, or more generally a negotiable instrument, that could be transferred from one person to another by endorsement. In England the presentment, demand, protest, or notice of dishonor of such negotiable instruments was handled by a Notary Public and thus these duties became the province of the Notary Public in America.

Early Responsibilities and Powers

The Constitution of the United States left the responsibility for the enactment of Notary laws to the individual states. Therefore, each state passed Notary laws based on the commercial interests, business needs, and customs of its citizens. For example, in those states where there was a harbor or port used by foreign vessels, the Notary was empowered to take maritime protest. A maritime protest is a form of affidavit made by a ship's captain to describe an accident, such as damage caused by a storm at sea that may have caused the ship to stop for repairs at an unscheduled port or otherwise delayed its arrival.

In the 1800's, it was not always possible to take the testimony of a witness in a courtroom. Transportation was slow and witnesses were often incapable of making an appearance for reasons of distance or, in some cases, health. Therefore, Notaries Public were empowered to take depositions. An attorney or judge would make up a set of questions that the Notary would submit to the witness. The Notary would write down the witness' replies, administer an oath to him, obtain his signature, and deliver the deposition, properly signed and sealed, to the court.

Notaries were also empowered at this time to take oaths and affidavits. These differed from depositions in that they were not always used in connection with court proceedings. Affidavits were required for such documents as creditors' bills, publication of delinquent tax lists, homestead claims, government claims for mineral lands, and government back pay and pensions.

As the states were surveyed and property became valuable, written agreements were needed for the conveyance or buying and selling of land. Notaries Public were authorized to take the acknowledgments of deeds, conveyances of land, mortgages, and other documents relating to real estate. It became the Notary's duty to identify the parties, witness their signatures (and private seals in some cases), obtain the parties' acknowledgment that the agreement be in full force and effect, and affix his official Notary seal and official signature to the certificate of acknowledgment.

In the nineteenth century, some of the states permitted or required the person whose signature was being notarized to use a private seal in lieu of or in addition to his signature on a document. If the person was unable to write, he was permitted to make an "X" as his mark or signature. Some states enacted laws prescribing the acknowledgment forms to be used by the Notary when a person signed his name with an "X." The private seal in that time was often called a scroll seal or scrawl and consisted of the written word "seal" or the letters "L.S." enclosed in loops or parentheses. The form varied according to the handwriting of the person whose signature was being notarized. The metal seal embosser as we know it today was not yet in use either as a private seal or an official notarial seal.

Slow transportation also led to the legal provision that a Notary be authorized to take proofs of acknowledgments. For example, if the party to sign a deed (the grantor) was unable to appear before the Notary, it was provided that one or more witnesses might appear before the Notary and certify under oath that they had seen the grantor sign the deed and that it was the grantor's intention that the deed should be in effect. These witnesses "proved" to the Notary that the document had been signed by the party as grantor. Today, proofs of acknowledgments are rarely necessary unless the party whose signature has been notarized has died or disappeared.

Until the office of the Recorder of Public Documents was established in the States, good business practice and often state law provided that the Notary keep a record book or register of his acknowledgments, or proofs of acknowledgments, of deeds as well as some of his other notarial acts. It should be noted that the Notary may often have kept the original document in his files and thus it was not necessary for him to record the details of the notarization in his record book. Most all states enacted laws requiring that a Notary make a certified copy of any document in his records for anyone upon payment of the proper fee. Because public recorders were few, and machines for making copies of documents did not exist, the notarial record book served a very different purpose than it does today.

At the time the states were framing constitutions and enacting Notary laws, it became necessary for them to appoint public officials with the power to perform notarial duties for absent citizens. These officers were called Commissioners of Deeds and they usually were appointed to act and reside in a state or territory where there were no Notaries Public. They were authorized to perform notarial acts in the foreign state or territory in which they lived for citizens of their home state who were also living in the foreign state or territory and who, for example, desired to deed property in their home state to another person. The Commissioners of Deeds are rarely known or used today.

The country of origin of the citizens of a state had an important influence on the kind of Notary laws that were enacted in that state. Those states whose inhabitants came originally from England tended to follow the English laws and customs in connection with the enactment of laws and statutes governing Notaries Public. Those states whose citizens came from Spain and France were also influenced by the customs and laws of the country of their origin. The French influence on Louisiana notarial laws, even today, enable a Notary in that state to perform many duties that in other states are considered to be the practice of law.

Enactment of Notary Laws

To conclude, the factors that have affected the enactment of Notary laws in the states vary according to the business needs of the community, the customs of business practice, and the country of origin of the citizens. In many cases Notary laws were not enacted until it proved necessary to control improper notarial practices. States that had little need for Notaries passed a minimum of Notary laws. In other states where few laws were enacted, notarial functions were based on good business practice and commercial usage. Advances in communications, transportation, and copying machines have now made it necessary to re-evaluate the purposes of and needs for Notaries Public in the United States.

QUESTIONS (Chapter 1)

1. What circumstances led to the use of the word "seal" in connection with Notary duties in Roman times?

2. What were the primary duties of a Notary Public during the Colonial period in the United States? Why?

3. How are laws governing Notaries enacted in the United States?

4. How were Notary records kept before the establishment of Recorders of Public Documents?

5. Who were Commissioners of Deeds and what did they do? Are they used today?

6. What is the origin of the word "Notary?"

7. What factors led to the enactment of Notary laws in the 1800's?

CHAPTER 2

The Need for Notarial Acts

What is A Notary Public?

A Notary Public is a citizen of high moral character and integrity, appointed by a local public official of his state, county, or territory to perform notarial acts of a nonlegal or ministerial nature in connection with both written and oral agreements. The Notary has either been trained to perform his notarial acts in connection with his principal occupation or acts under the supervision and guidance of an attorney. The official duties, powers, and functions of a Notary Public are confined to

1. Determining positively and beyond the shadow of a doubt that the party or parties to a written agreement are the party or parties they claim to be.
2. Obtaining the acknowledgment of the party or parties to an agreement that he, she, or they have signed the agreement or taken oath that they are aware of the contents of the agreement.
3. Applying and affixing a distinguishing mark or seal (in addition to his official signature) to ensure as fully as possible that the original agreement cannot later be altered, blanks filled in, or pages added or eliminated, either intentionally or

unintentionally, by the parties to the agreement or anyone else after the document has been notarized.

4. Making a written record of his act of notarization in an official record book kept by him for that purpose, regardless of whether such record is described or required by state law.

QUESTIONS (Chapter 2)

1. In what ways (other than education) do the duties, responsibilities and obligations of a Notary Public differ from those of an attorney?

2. What are four primary responsibilities of the Notary Public?

3. Why are the responsibilities and duties of the Notary in the 20th Century different from those in the 1800's?

CHAPTER 3

The Importance of Notarization

Notarization Defined

A notarization is a written statement, also called a certificate or certification, to which a Notary Public has affixed his official signature, official seal embosser, title, jurisdiction, commission expiration date, and address. The certificate generally states that a person or persons voluntarily (1) appeared before the Notary, (2) took an oath or affidavit and/or signed an agreement or statement, (3) acknowledged to the Notary that they signed the agreement or took the oath. Notarizations are performed by Notaries Public in connection with oaths, affirmations, affidavits, depositions, acknowledgments, and any other acts that Notaries are empowered to perform by virtue of state law or custom.

Why Notarization is Necessary

A document is notarized so that the parties to an agreement can assure each other that this particular document (and no other) is the authentic document and as such contains the particular agreement intended to be in full force and effect. If the document has been notarized properly and subsequently recorded in the public record, it may be easily distinguished from another seemingly identical document. After the Notary has affixed his official signature and official seal to his certification on the document, it may be recorded in the public record; and this gives notice to the public that this particular agreement is intended to be in full force and effect.

Photocopying Machines and Seal Embossers

Recent improvements in photocopying machines make it even more important that a document be notarized and that it be notarized properly. For example, a notarized and recorded document could be machine copied with alterations. If the altered copy were recorded in the public record, there would be two supposedly authentic recorded documents. Which of the two would be the authentic document that was intended to be in full force and effect by the parties concerned?

It thus becomes evident that in order to reduce the possibility of illegal, or even unintentional, alterations of an authentic original document, the Notary should make some mark on or in each page of the document that cannot be photocopied. The effectiveness of a notarization can be increased immeasurably if the Notary has used an official seal embosser, which makes indentations into the paper of the document that cannot be photographed. The Notary should provide himself with an official seal embosser that is not identical with any other Notary's official seal embosser. Obviously, nothing would be accomplished if the indentations made by all official seal embossers were the same. The official seal embosser should contain the Notary's name, as well as any state required information, and should always be kept in a safe place.

QUESTIONS (Chapter 3)

1. What identifying information, in addition to the Notary's signature and seal, should be entered on a certificate?

2. What purpose is served by having a document notarized and made a public record?

3. What is a seal embosser and why is it an important instrument to the Notary Public?

4. What modern business machine, more than any other, has made the need for proper notarization so important?

5. What are the three statements contained in most notarial certificates?

6. Why should a seal embosser contain the Notary's name?

CHAPTER 4

Powers and Functions

Acknowledgment Defined

In the United States, the word "acknowledgment" is used to mean a "certificate of acknowledgment," which is a written statement signed by a Notary. Acknowledgment is also used to mean an "act of acknowledgment," which is the act of recognition, or admission of the existence, of an agreement made by the party whose signature is notarized.

The certificate of acknowledgment is a legal form, and has been specified in some state codes. If it is not specified in state code, it should be formulated by an attorney. The Notary who is not an attorney should rely on printed forms of acknowledgment or on the advice of an attorney. The average Notary is not qualified or empowered to draft, or advise others, on the form or kind of certificate of acknowledgment that should be used. In most cases, however, the person requesting notarization will provide the Notary with the proper certificate of acknowledgment, so that the Notary need only perform his notarial act in exact compliance with the statement in the certificate of acknowledgment.

The Acknowledgment Certificate

The general form of certificate of acknowledgment, as it is used in most states today, can be broken down into the following parts:

1. The Venue: *State of* _____, *County of* _____, *SS.* This is a statement of the location where the Notary is performing his notarial act. It does not necessarily refer to the location where the instrument was written or signed by the party, or where it is to be recorded, or where the Notary is commissioned to act. The letters "SS." are an abbreviation of the Latin word "scilicet," meaning "namely," "to wit," or "more particularly described as." It was used in old English documents to designate the particular place within a city or county in England where the Notary or official was performing his act. The SS. would follow the statement of the state, for example, *State of* _____, *SS.* (meaning more particularly) *the County of* _____. American printers probably retained the SS. on the certificate to balance the Venue line for the sake of appearance only. Today the abbreviation SS. is falling into disuse, as locations are now well defined in the United States and it no longer serves a purpose.

2. The Date of the Acknowledgment: *On the* _____ *day of* _____, *19*_____. .... In this space the Notary should insert the date he signed the certificate. This can become a very important date, and the Notary must be especially careful that he is actually inserting the correct date. If the Notary deems it important, he can also include the day of the week and the hour he signs. It should be pointed out that the date of the acknowledgment is not necessarily the date the document was signed by the parties or the date of the agreement between the parties.

3. The Name, Title, and Jurisdiction of the Notary:

. . . before me, John Jones, a Notary Public in and for the state of _____ . . . . This phrase need not appear at this place, as it is generally given following the Notary's signature. The spaces should be filled in, however, if they are printed on the certificate.

4. Presence of the Signer: . . . *personally came or appeared before me.* . . . If the person whose signature is notarized did not appear before the Notary, the Notary is signing a false statement. A certificate of acknowledgment cannot be taken over the telephone if the certificate states that the person "appeared before" the Notary.

5. Name of the Signer or Signers: The name of the signer may be inserted here in the blank space of two or three lines provided on most printed forms. If the Notary himself is required to insert the names of the signers, he must be careful to see that the names on the agreement agree exactly with the names he inserts in the blank spaces provided on his certificate. If the signer's middle name is abbreviated on the agreement, the Notary should also abbreviate it when he inserts it on the certificate. The names of all parties to the agreement (including those whose signatures are *not* being notarized) should be signed, written or printed, in exactly the same way that they appear on all places on the document.

If only one name is to be inserted in a blank space, say of three lines, the Notary should be careful to draw a line through the remaining two blank spaces, so that there will be no chance that another name or names will be added to the certificate at a later date.

Identifying the Signer

6. Identification of the Signer: . . . *to me known or known to me to be the person or persons described in and who executed the foregoing or within instrument.* If a person is unknown to the Notary, there is absolutely no

positive identification that he can present to the Notary to prove his identity. The question of whether a person is known to the Notary or unknown to the Notary must be decided in a court of law. Each case of "known vs. unknown" will vary depending on the degree of diligence, competence, skill, and integrity of the Notary. It will also depend upon the kind of agreement and the form of acknowledgment that was used.

A U.S. Passport is probably the best kind of identification that a person can present to a Notary, but, of course, not everyone has a passport. Until a few years ago drivers' licenses were considered satisfactory as identification, but photocopying machines have now made it easy for such licenses to be forged in states where the official seal is not embossed or perforated into the license itself. The Notary should always take notice of the kind of official seal that appears on all items of identification presented to him by the signer. If the identification card is printed on expensive paper or specially made paper (with a water mark, for example), it will be more difficult to forge identification. A few states have allowed the state seal to be affixed to the drivers' license with a rubber stamp. By changing his date of birth on his driver's license and obtaining a photocopy of the altered original, the juvenile uses the fraudulent license as proof of age to obtain intoxicating beverages. The photograph and even the signature on such a driver's license could be substituted, photocopied, and the resulting forgery presented to the unwary Notary as proof of the identity of a signer.

Also helpful in identifying a party's signature is a comparison of all the signatures made by that party in the Notary's presence with those on his identification cards. These signatures should, of course, be compared with the signature on the document.

The Notary who keeps a careful and detailed official record book or journal will lessen his chances of being involved in a case of "known vs. unknown." An impersonator will be reluctant to sign a false name in the Notary's record book or give the Notary a false address that the Notary not only enters in his official record book but might check later.

When a Notary accepts the identification presented by a party, he should consider that he is in effect signing his name as an indemnitor to a note or cashing a large check for the party, as he will be held liable if any person sustains damages as a result of his failure to properly identify the signer.

The certificate of acknowledgment may state " _____, known to me to be the President of the Jones Corporation and the Secretary of the Jones Corporation . . ." or " _____, known to me to be the attorney-in-fact for John Jones. . . ." The Notary who is not an attorney, or who is not acting under the supervision of an attorney, should be very cautious in signing his name to the certificate if he is not positively sure that the person is actually the person described (President, Secretary, or attorney-in-fact) in the certificate and in the document.

Acknowledgment is Made Freely and Voluntarily

7. Voluntary Acknowledgment: . . . *and he, she, or they acknowledged to me that he, she or they executed the same.* It is necessary for the signer to admit or recognize or acknowledge to the Notary that he is aware of the terms and existence of the agreement that he has signed. The acknowledgment is voluntary, as opposed to involuntary, in that it is made freely and willingly to the Notary in contrast to an agreement that the signer has been coerced or forced to sign.

8. Testimonium Clause: *In witness whereof, I have hereunto set my hand and official seal this* _____ *day of* _____, *19* _____. Or a shorter form: *Witness my hand and seal*. The date need not be repeated if it was already inserted in the Date of the Acknowledgment section of the certificate. A blank line is usually placed under the Testimonium Clause for the signature of the Notary. State laws vary with regard to the information that a Notary is instructed to place after his signature and also whether an official seal is required. Good business practice, however, dictates that the Notary use an official seal embosser and print (a rubber stamp is preferred) below his signature the following information: his title (Notary Public), his jurisdiction (in and for the State of _____), his commission expiration date (My commission expires _____), and the street address, city, and state where his office is located.

If the Notary's certificate of acknowledgment is stapled to the document, the Notary should squeeze the document and the certificate together with his official seal embosser. The placement of the Notary's official seal embosser is discussed in the section on official seal embossers.

Proofs of Acknowledgment

Proof of acknowledgment is taken by a Notary when the party who made the acknowledgment did not appear and cannot now appear before the Notary or when the party can appear before the Notary but is not personally known to the Notary. A witness or witnesses are required to take an oath administered by the Notary, who completes a special form of certificate. The rules, laws, and forms required or prescribed vary from state to state and in most states these laws are very strict. The Proof of

Acknowledgment form is rarely used today because it is easy to find a Notary. If the Notary takes a proof that later proves to be invalid, he can be held liable to all persons who sustain damages as a result of his improper notarial act. Unless he is an attorney, the Notary is also taking a risk of unlawfully engaging in the practice of law, if he does not follow the proper legal procedure or use the proper proof form.

Signature By Mark

In the 1800's some states passed laws specifying the form of a certificate of acknowledgment (and the required witnesses) when a party was unable to sign his name. Today, a person who cannot write probably cannot read and therefore would be unable to read the agreement he was to sign using a mark such as an "X." It is very rare that a person who is capable of becoming a party to an important agreement is unable to write his name.

Occasionally the Notary may be asked to take the acknowledgement of a person who is unable to write his name or appears to be mentally incompetent and incapable of understanding and acknowledging to the Notary that he realizes the importance of the document and intends that it be placed in effect. If there is any question of the mental or physical competence of the party whose signature is to be notarized, the Notary who is not an attorney should always obtain legal advice before taking unnecessary chances, which could result in his being involved in long drawn-out lawsuits.

Absentee Voter's Ballot

Many of the states have enacted statutes enabling a Notary, or other qualified public officer, to certify to and take the oath of a person who is temporarily not living in his home state during an election. The envelope that contains the ballot itself usually has both an affidavit to be signed by the voter and a certificate to be signed by the Notary printed on the outside of the envelope. The oath to be administered by the Notary and affidavit to be signed by the voter may read as follows:

I *(Insert name of voter),* do solemnly swear that I am a registered voter in the city or town of _____, county of _____, ward of _____, precinct number _____: that I have carefully read the instructions herein enclosed, that I have marked, enclosed and sealed the within ballot as stated hereon by the person taking my oath; and that I have marked said ballot within, and that I will mail it at a Post Office situated in the city or town of _____ in the state or country of _____. *(Voter signs here.)*

The above affidavit is generally followed by the Notary's certificate, which may read as follows:

Subscribed and sworn to before me by the above affiant, personally known to me or identified to my satisfaction, this _____ day of _____, 19____, in the city or town of _____, state of _____, and country of _____. I hereby certify that when I was alone with the affiant he showed me the ballot herein enclosed, unmarked, and then in my presence marked the same without my seeing how he marked it, after which he sealed said ballot in this envelope. I had no communication with the affiant as to how he was to vote. *(Here Notary signs his name, title, etc. and affixes his seal.)*

Before the Notary signs the certificate, he must take all precautions to ensure that, if the voter is not personally known to him, he is properly identified, as specified on the Notary's certificate.

Oaths, Affirmations, and Affidavits

The Notary in most states is authorized and empowered to administer oaths, affirmations, and affidavits. An oath is a solemn pledge or promise made by a person (often called the affiant) with an appeal to God, or a Supreme Being, to attest to the truth of his words. An affidavit is a similar pledge or statement that has been put in writing and signed by the affiant. The Notary adds his certification (known as a "jurat"), which states that the person appeared before him, took the oath, and signed the affidavit.

State laws vary on the exact form of oath that the Notary should administer to the affiant and also on the manner in which the Notary should administer the oath. In all cases, however, the Notary must respect the solemnity of an oath and insist that the affiant either raise his right hand or place it on the Bible before he administers the oath. A typical oath of office that is taken by a Notary is as follows:

You do solemnly swear (or affirm) that you will support the Constitution of the United States and the Constitution of the State of _____ so long as you continue a citizen thereof, and that you will faithfully discharge, according to law, the duties of the office of Notary Public to the best of your ability, so help you God.

The person to whom the oath has been administered answers "I do." Because the word "swear" is not permitted in some religions the word "affirm" has been substituted. Thus the term "affirmation" on occasion replaces the word "oath."

Oaths and affirmations are also administered by public officials and Notaries Public with regard to depositions and in court trials. The Notary without special training and education in connection with his principal occupation will not be called on to administer these oaths.

There are two general forms of jurat (or certification) used by Notaries Public for affidavits. In all cases before administering the oath in connection with an affidavit, the Notary should ask the affiant either to raise his right hand or to place it on the Bible. The oath can be administered as follows: "You do solemnly swear (or affirm) that the statements made in this affidavit are the truth, the whole truth, and nothing but the truth, so help you God." The affiant answers "I do."

The short form of the certificate or jurat, which is written after the signature of the affiant on the affidavit, reads:

Subscribed and sworn to before me this _____ day of _____, 19____.

The second form, which is longer, is also used in some states, and reads:

Be it known that on this _____ day of _____, 19____, before me _____, a Notary Public for the State of _____, residing in the city of _____ in said county, duly commissioned and sworn, and by law authorized to administer oaths and affirmations, personally appeared _____, the affiant of the County of _____, to me well known, and known to be the person he represents himself to be, who, being by me duly sworn, did make the following (or foregoing) affidavit by him subscribed. In testimony whereof, I have hereunto set my hand and affixed my seal of office the day and year first above written.

The Notary then signs the jurat and prints or

stamps his name, title, jurisdiction, commission expiration date, and address. The Notary should impress his official seal embosser over the letters "L.S.," as explained in the section on official seals.

The Notary who is not an attorney should not draw or prepare the actual affidavit itself unless he is acting under the direction or supervision of an attorney. The Notary is only concerned with the absolute truth of the certificate (jurat) that he signs. It should be noted that in the two sample jurats given above there is an important difference. In the second example, or longer form, the Notary is certifying to the fact that he knows the affiant, and he must therefore exercise the same cautions that he would in an acknowledgment, that is, be positively certain that the affiant is known to him without the shadow of a doubt.

Though it may not be required by state law, the Notary should make a written record of his notarial act of administering an oath, affirmation, or affidavit. How he should record those entries that apply to oaths, affirmations, and affidavits is explained in the section on record books.

Certified Copies

During the 1800's most states enacted laws requiring that a Notary make and give a certified copy of any of his official records to anyone requesting a copy and paying the proper fee. At that time the office of Recorder of Public Documents as we know it today had not become established. Neither was it possible to run off machine copies of a document. The Notary was often called upon to copy by hand a document that he held for safekeeping in his files or one that was brought to his office. After making the copy, the Notary would write, sign, and seal a statement or certification on the copy to the effect that he had carefully compared the original and copy and found the copy to be a full, accurate, true, and correct copy of the original.

Today most important documents are recorded in the office of the Recorder of Public Documents who is obligated to furnish a certified copy of any public record to anyone paying the proper fee. The Recorder's Office is usually equipped with every conceivable kind of machine for making copies of documents. Therefore, the Notary is now rarely called upon for this service. If asked to give a certified copy of a document that has been recorded in the public record, the Notary should always refer the party to the Recorder of Public Documents.

Occasionally a Notary may be asked to furnish a certified copy (which requires his signature and official seal) of a document that has not been recorded in the public record. Because of the ease with which an original authentic document may be altered and photocopied, either before the document is presented to the Notary or after the certified copy with the Notary's signature and official seal leaves his office, the Notary should avoid if possible furnishing certified copies. If the Notary finds that he is obligated to make a certified copy for a party, he should always hold in his files a facsimile of the document he has certified, so it may be compared if necessary at a later date with the alleged original. The Notary should not furnish certified copies of documents unless he has assured himself that such copies cannot be obtained from a Recorder of Public Documents and the preparation of such copies is not against the law. Certified copies of birth certificates should not be furnished by a Notary and it is against U.S. law for anyone to make copies of U.S. Passports.

Negotiable Instruments and Depositions

During the 1800's most Notaries Public were authorized and empowered by law to perform certain acts and duties in connection with the notarization of negotiable instruments and depositions. Today, these notarial acts are generally considered to fall within the province of the practice of law and banking. Not only have laws regarding negotiable instruments changed but also custom and practice. In most states, the Notary laws have not been brought up to date to reflect the changes that have occurred in the banking industry and in negotiable instruments law. In years gone by, whole sections of Notary books were devoted to the explanation of many legal terms and forms relating to the presentment, demand, protest, and notice of dishonor of negotiable instruments. Today, the average Notary will never be called upon to perform such notarial acts.

Depositions are, of course, still in use and form a very important part of a witness' testimony that is taken outside of court. The act of taking a deposition, or notarizing the jurat in connection with a deposition, is performed by Notaries Public who are attorneys or who have had special training in connection with their principal occupation.

QUESTIONS (Chapter 4)

1. Is a Notary obliged to advise others what form of acknowledgment is to be used? Why?

2. Why is it so important for a Notary to have the party for whom a document is being notarized also sign in the Notary's record book?

3. Is it always necessary for a signer of a document to appear before the Notary Public? Why?

4. What is considered the best evidence of identity? Why?

5. How does an oath differ from an affirmation?

6. What is a "Recorder of Public Documents" and what does he do?

7. What should a Notary keep in his possession when he gives a party a certified copy of a document? Why?

8. What is an affidavit? How is it different from an oath?

9. What is a jurat? Is it signed by the Notary?

CHAPTER 5

Procedures

Official Signature and Testimonium Clause

The statement or certification to which the Notary signs his name and affixes his official seal is the essence or "reason for being" of the notarization. The Notary must carefully read the jurat or certificate of acknowledgment that he is about to sign to be absolutely sure that he is not signing a false certificate.

The Testimonium Clause on the certificate of acknowledgment or jurat states generally "Witness my hand and seal," or sometimes, if a seal is not required by law in that state, simply "Witness my hand." This Testimonium Clause is a pledge made by the Notary that he has read the certificate of acknowledgment or jurat that he is signing and sealing and complied with its terms.

The signature of the Notary should be legible. Some years ago there was a tendency toward writing illegibly on purpose, because illegible signatures were difficult to copy or forge. But today the photocopying machine can provide a copy of a signature that is almost impossible to tell from the original. Also it is more difficult to compare a possible forged signature with the authentic one if it was originally written illegibly.

After his signature or under his signature, the Notary should legibly write, print, or rubber stamp (the latter is preferred) his name as he signed it, his title and jurisdiction *(Notary Public in and for the State of _____)*, the date of expiration of his notarial commission, and the address where his office or residence is located. A rubber stamp containing this information is more efficient and will take up less space on the document than if it is printed by hand or typed.

Official Seal Embosser

A seal embosser is a plier-like device with a metal grip or handle. Its jaws consist of male and female round metal or plastic dies on which are engraved a legend, which usually includes the name of the Notary, his title and jurisdiction, and the coat of arms of his state. When a piece of paper is inserted between the jaws and the handle squeezed, the male and female dies are pressed together, causing indentations to be made in the paper that reproduce the legend engraved on the dies.

The most important purpose of a seal embosser is to make indentations into the paper of the document so that the indentations cannot be photocopied or easily duplicated (except by using the same seal embosser that was employed originally). Because the indentations cannot be machine copied, it is difficult to forge an authentic original by passing an altered copy off as an original. The U.S. Passport, for example, has the indentations of the Seal of the United States impressed over the photograph of the holder of the passport. The U.S. Seal first of all authenticates the passport and makes it official. Second, it reduces the possibility that an unauthorized person could make an effective forgery. (It is, of course, unlawful to attempt to copy, or furnish a copy of, a passport or any certificate of naturalization.)

A Notary Public uses an official seal embosser as a

means of protecting the public against persons who might unlawfully try to alter a notarized, authentic original document and pass it off as an original. With the advent of the photocopiers, by which duplicates are made in a few seconds, it has become even more important for a Notary to provide himself with an official seal embosser, regardless of whether one is required by state law.

Custom and commercial usage also seem to indicate that the public at large expects a Notary to use an official seal embosser because it has become accepted as the official seal or mark that verifies that the agreement has been notarized.

Photocopying Machines and Forgery

In the 1800's it was still a tedious matter to make a copy of a document. Before the office of the Recorder of Public Documents was established, the Notary often kept the original agreement in his possession. No copies were available unless they were made in longhand by the Notary on payment of his fee. The photocopying machines available today in the United States make it possible to reproduce such an exact copy of an original document that it is very difficult to distinguish the original from a copy. Only the indentations made by the Notary's official seal embosser cannot be machine copied.

However, forgeries and fraudulent copies of original, authentic notarized documents are not prevented by the Notary's use of an official seal embosser. Though the Notary may have used an official seal embosser, it is still possible for the authentic originally notarized document to be altered before it is recorded in the public record. What is important is that the document should go directly to the Recorder's Office after it is notarized so that unauthorized persons will not have the opportunity to attempt to make fraudulent copies before the document is recorded in the public record. In many cases, however, this is not possible; the document is usually returned to the person who has asked for the notarization. Obviously the possibility of a forgery or an altered copy is vastly reduced if the Notary has affixed his official seal embosser to the document. The Notary who makes and keeps a detailed official record book (as explained in the section on record books) of all his notarial acts at the same time as he performs the notarial acts will also lessen the temptation of a forger to make fraudulent copies. If the Notary has used an official seal embosser and has made a detailed record of his notarial act, there can be no question of whether he has performed his act with the necessary diligence, skill, and competence, by virtue of his oath of office and the conditions of his Notary bond.

How and Where to Use the Seal Embosser
The Notary should impress his official seal embosser in the 2 by 2-inch blank space (if provided) to the left of the Notary's certificate. Many printed certificate forms and legal forms, however, do not provide blank space for the official seal. The Notary is then obligated to impress his official seal in a space near the signature (or signatures) of the party (or parties) whose signature was notarized. Before applying his seal embosser, either in the blank space provided or anywhere else on the document, the Notary should carefully print the letters "L.S." in the center of the place where he intends to squeeze his official seal embosser. The letters "L.S." are an abbreviation for the Latin words *locus sigilli*, which mean "the location where the seal is placed." It should again be noted that the official seal embosser is used

because its indentation cannot be reproduced. The original, authentic notarized document can be easily distinguished from a machine-made copy, which does not show the indentations made by the Notary's official seal embosser. The Notary should always print the letters "L.S." in the place over which he squeezes his seal embosser. The conformity of the letters "L.S." will be changed by the indentations made by the seal embosser so that a machine-made copy will show up the change in the alignment of the letters, making it evident that an official seal embosser was used on the original, authentic notarized document.

The Notary may find that there is no blank space on the document large enough to place the whole impression of his seal embosser. If there is a margin, the Notary should print the letters "L.S." over which he applies as much of his official seal as there is space for. This is preferable to no seal at all. If there is neither margin nor blank space, the Notary will be obliged to affix his seal embosser's impression in a place on the document where there is printed rather than written or typewritten material. The indentations of the seal on the written part of a document may make the writing illegible, and though this might aid in preventing forgeries, the document means nothing if it cannot be read.

In some states a separate printed form of a certificate of acknowledgment is being made available to Notaries Public, who staple these certificates to the document. Some of these loose certificates provide a space for the official seal embosser. The disadvantages of loose certificates are discussed in the next section on record books. If a loose certificate is stapled to the document, the Notary should print the letters "L.S." between the staples on the margin and then squeeze the document and stapled certificate together with his seal embosser. The Notary should also print "L.S." and affix his seal on the certificate itself (if space is provided) as well as on the document to which the certificate is attached. If there is no space available on the document itself for the seal embosser, the Notary should use the margins as explained above. If the document consists of more than one page, it would be well for the Notary to write the letters "L.S." and squeeze a portion of his seal embosser on the margin of each page, in addition to the page on which his certificate appears or is stapled.

Rubber Stamp Seal

A seal embosser has been described as a metal device whose indentations, appearing on a document, help to indicate that the document was notarized and also help identify the Notary. Because many Notaries were not careful to print their name, title, jurisdiction, expiration date, and address legibly on all documents they notarized, a few states have enacted laws that require Notaries to put some or all of this information on a rubber stamp, called a "rubber stamp seal." An official seal embosser should always be used in addition to the rubber stamp seal. In order to make the indentations of the embosser legible for photographic reproduction, it is possible to blacken the indentations by rubbing them with carbon paper or by pressing them with an inked blank rubber stamp.

Even if the Notary has used an official seal embosser (or a seal embosser and a rubber stamp seal), he should, in all events, avoid indicating or describing on the document or his certificate how he has affixed his seal. To be avoided is the use of any printed or rubber stamped description (other than the letters "L.S.") that indicates how the document was notarized, such as "Notary has affixed official seal on original" or "This is an authentic original if it bears the signature or seal of the Notary in purple ink." It is obvious that such a descriptive statement can easily be eliminated by a forger from the fraudulent copy. It is also easy to alter the word "purple" to read "black" or any other color to suit the photocopying machine the forger is using. A descriptive statement is especially hazardous when the Notary has not used any seal at all or has used a rubber stamp seal.

Regardless of whether it is required by state law, good business practice, custom, and commercial usage require that every Notary provide himself with an official seal embosser as well as a rubber stamp containing his name, title, jurisdiction, expiration date, and address.

The Notary's official seal embosser should always be kept in a safe place where it cannot be picked up and used by unauthorized persons. It should be destroyed or surrendered to the public official in charge of Notaries when the Notary resigns, is removed from office, permits his commission to expire, or dies.

Record Book of Official Acts (Journal)

State statutes vary widely with reference to the Notary's register or record book. Some states require that a "fair and just record" be made and kept by the Notary, but they do not describe what is "fair and just"; others describe the entries required that pertain to certain official acts; and still others fail to even mention a record book. A few states have enacted laws requiring a Journal of Notarial Acts as described in the Uniform Notary Act. (See Appendix A.)

The Notary who makes and keeps a detailed chronological record of his official acts (and uses an official seal embosser) demonstrates to all who need his services that he understands the importance of his notarial act. Most lawsuits for damages against Notaries could have been avoided if the Notary had kept a record book and used an official seal embosser.

Every Notary Public who has taken the oath of office of Notary has a responsibility to those he serves, as a capable and competent person, to discharge his notarial acts with diligence and skill as well as honesty and integrity. A Notary is called on to perform his act because of the importance or special significance of a document or oath. The party requesting the notarization has come before the Notary because he wants his oath or acknowledgment to have special significance, and because his oath, or the agreement he is making, is a solemn pledge that he intends to abide by the terms expressed in his oath or agreement. It is, therefore, the obligation of every Notary to make an official chronological record of all his notarial acts, regardless of whether such a record is required or described by state law.

Entries in the Record Book (Journal)

A checklist of entries to be inserted by the Notary in his record book could include some or all of the following items:

1. Date and time of official act.
2. Date of document or agreement.
3. Date parties signed.
4. Notarial fees for act and recording of act.
5. Kind of official act (acknowledgment, oath, etc.).
6. Kind of document (grant deed, etc.).
7. Names and addresses (printed) of parties whose signatures were notarized.
8. Signatures of parties whose signatures were notarized in Notary's record book.

9. Kinds of identification (including card numbers) presented by parties whose signatures were notarized.
10. Number of pages in document.
11. Whether all pages of document and corrections were initialed by the Notary and all parties.
12. Whether all blanks were filled in on the document.
13. Whether a loose certificate or jurat was stapled to the document.
14. Whether an official seal embosser was used.
15. Description or location of property.
16. Names and addresses (printed) of parties whose signatures were NOT notarized.
17. Names and addresses (printed) of witnesses, if any.
18. Signatures of witnesses and kinds of identification presented by them, if any.
19. Any other entries required by law in this state.

Item 1. The date and time of the Notary's official act may become very important if several similar instruments are subsequently recorded in the office of the Recorder of Public Documents. The Notary's entry in his record book of the exact time the acknowledgment was taken by him could help establish which of two similar documents was the authentic original and which was the altered machine-made copy.

Items 2 and 3. The date of the document or agreement and the date the parties signed need not always be the same. The parties may have signed the agreement several days before coming to the Notary, and during this time they may have signed other similar agreements. But the moment they appear before the Notary, the parties will have agreed that this one particular document among all others is the document that shall be in effect.

Item 4. The fee charged by the Notary should take into account the fee for the performance of the notarial act, as well as the fee for making and keeping a proper record book of the details of the notarial act. Schedules of notarial fees have not been revised for many years in most states. They do not take into account the increased cost of living, the increased cost of transportation (if the Notary must go to the person whose signature is being notarized), and also the skill and time that is necessary to make a written record of the details of the Notary's official act. A few states have enacted laws to the effect that a Notary may not charge a fee for notarial acts performed for persons applying for U.S. Government benefits, pensions, charity, or public assistance. There is no state that requires the Notary to charge a fee for his services, if he decides he wants to perform these services free of charge.

Items 5 and 6. The record book will not, of course, be complete unless the kind of official act and the kind of document are noted.

Item 7. Good business practice dictates that the names and addresses of the parties whose signatures were notarized should be printed in the record book.

Items 8 and 9. The Notary should require the person whose signature has been notarized on the document to also sign his name in the Notary's record book. The importance of this entry, as well as the entry on the kind of identification presented by the person whose signature was notarized, cannot be overemphasized. In taking the acknowledgment of a party, the Notary is certifying that the party is personally known to be the person described in the document and that this person is signing the document voluntarily. Impersonators will not be inclined to sign a false name in the Notary's record book if they know that the Notary keeps the record book in his possession as proof of signature and identification if it is ever questioned. Many suits for damages could have been avoided if the Notary had obtained the signature of the person appearing before him in his record book and had also recorded the kind of identification the party furnished to prove his identity. A good official record book can be used as evidence of the Notary's diligent and skillful performance of his notarial act in compliance with his oath of office and the conditions of his Notary bond and Notary's Errors and Omissions Insurance Policy. (See the section on this policy.)

After the Notary has obtained the signature of the party in his record book, he should carefully compare that signature with the signature on the document to assure himself that both signatures were made by the same party, who is the party appearing before him. The signatures should also correspond exactly with the printed or typewritten name of the party as it appears on the document. For example, if a middle initial is given on the document, the Notary should see that the signature also includes the middle initial.

Items 10 and 11. If the document contains more than one page, the Notary should count the number of pages in the document and record the number in his record book. The Notary should also see that all pages are securely stapled or tied together. All parties to the agreement, including the Notary, should place their initials in the lower right-hand corner of each page of the document. If the document is particularly important, the Notary may also place a partial impression of his official seal embosser over the letters "L.S." in the margin of each page. This will help avoid the possibility of pages being added or eliminated after the document has left the office of the Notary. It will also provide additional protection in case illegally altered copies appear later.

If it is necessary to make any corrections on the document, the corrections should be made by one of the parties to the agreement and not by the Notary himself, except under the direction of an attorney. It is preferable for the agreement to be redrafted if too many corrections are necessary. The Notary and all parties to the agreement should initial any corrections in the margin opposite the correction. If the Notary makes a mistake in his notarial certificate and corrects it, he and all the parties should also initial the correction.

Item 12. At the time that the Notary verifies that all corrections on the document have been initialed, he should also check to make sure that the parties have filled in all blank spaces on the document. When a document is drafted, spaces are often left blank to enable the parties to insert such items as dates and amounts that are not known in advance. Unless the Notary is an attorney, he should not allow himself to be put in the position of an advisor or counselor to a party who does not know what should be inserted in the blank spaces on the document. The Notary should check, however, to see that all blank spaces are filled in or a line drawn through the blank space if it is not filled in. This is to ensure that a blank space will not be used to add information after the document has left the Notary's office.

Item 13. Most documents are printed or prepared so that the Notary's certificate will appear on the last page under the signature of the parties to the agreement. Sometimes, however, the Notary must provide a loose printed form of certificate, which is stapled to the document. The loose certificate should be stapled to the margins only, and the staples should not impair the legibility of any part of the document. The staples should be placed so that the certificate can be folded back by the

Recorder when the document is recorded to ensure that any writing or printing under the certificate will also be made a part of the public record. If a loose certificate is stapled to the document, the Notary should take care to see that all parties to the agreement have also initialed the lower right-hand corner of the certificate. The use of stapled certificates is not advisable if it can be avoided, because of the chances of other fraudulent certificates being substituted for the original merely by removing the staples and substituting another certificate. The use of the official seal embosser provides some additional protection for the parties against illegal alterations and substitutions of certificates.

Item 14. The correct placement of the official seal embosser on the document or a loose certificate and the reasons why the seal embosser is used are explained in the section on official seal embossers.

Item 15. The description or location of the property may be noted in the record book if the Notary considers it necessary, or if required by state law.

Item 16. Occasionally, when a Notary is asked to notarize a document for one party, he will notice that a notarization is also required for several other parties who have not appeared before the Notary. Of course, the Notary cannot notarize the signatures of these other parties. However, in such a case, it is important that the Notary record the names and addresses (if they are available) of those parties to the agreement whose signatures were NOT notarized. This reduces the possibility of the later addition to the Notary's certificate of the name of a party who did not appear before the Notary or the illegal substitution of a notarial certificate after the document has left the Notary's office.

Items 17 and 18. Depending on the kind of notarial act to be performed, the Notary may consider it necessary to record the names, addresses, and kinds of identification presented by the witnesses who appeared before him. It is also wise to obtain a sample of the witnesses' signatures in the Notary's record book. These entries would be required when a proof of an acknowledgment is taken.

Item 19. In this entry may be included miscellaneous information that pertains to the Notary's state.

If a photocopier is available and the party does not object, the Notary may make a photocopy of the notarized document. The Notary should keep this photocopy as a supplementary file to his notarial record of the act. If the document is presented as evidence in a court of law at a later date, the Notary will then be able to provide his photocopy to prove the document was not altered after it was notarized. Making a photocopy does not avoid the need to make a proper notarial record, or to have the document recorded in the public record.

In the event that a Notary resigns, fails to renew his notarial commission, vacates his office, is removed from his office, or dies, his official record book and his official seal embosser should be forwarded to the city, county, or state office responsible for keeping records of Notaries Public.

Summary of Practices

1. The Notary's signature should be written in ink in his own hand. (A rubber stamp with the Notary's signature should never be stamped on a notarial certificate.)
2. The Notary's name, title, jurisdiction, commission expiration date, and office or residence address should be carefully and legibly printed on all documents he notarizes. (A small rubber stamp is preferable.)

3. The Notary's official seal embosser should be used to make an indentation into the paper of all documents notarized. The seal embosser should be engraved with the Notary's name, the words "Notary Public," the state or county in which the Notary is commissioned to act, as well as any other information that is required by Notary law. (If a rubber stamp seal is permitted or required in the Notary's state, the Notary should always use his official seal embosser in addition to the rubber stamp seal.)

4. The Notary should make a systematic and detailed written record of all his notarial acts. He should obtain the signatures in his record book of all parties for whom he performs a notarization.

5. When taking an acknowledgment, the Notary should require the parties whose signatures he is notarizing to present to him satisfactory evidence of their identity. The Notary should make and keep a written record of the description of the kind of identification presented to him as well as the names and addresses of the parties.

6. Copies of a notarized document should not be signed by the Notary. Copies should be conformed and the word "copy" should be printed in large letters over the face of the document. The Notary should affix his seal and print or type his name, in the space provided for his signature, on the copy.

QUESTIONS (Chapter 5)

1. What is the purpose of a Testimonium Clause?

2. What is the difference between a Notary seal embosser and a Notary rubber stamp seal?

3. What do the letters "L.S." mean? Where and why are they written by the Notary?

4. Why is it important to obtain the signature in the Notary's record book of the party for whom the Notary has notarized a document?

5. How does a seal embosser help to prevent forgeries?

6. Why should a seal embosser always be used in addition to a rubber stamp seal in those states where a rubber stamp seal law has been enacted?

7. How does the Notary protect himself and the public by keeping a Notary's record book that has many more entries than those required by the Notary laws of his state?

8. What is considered to be the best evidence of a person's identity? Why?

CHAPTER 6

Limitations and Obligations

The Practice of Law

When a Notary accepts his commission as a Notary Public in the United States, he is in effect making a public announcement that he is an official of high moral character and integrity, who will and can perform his notarial acts skillfully and diligently, competently and faithfully, and in conformance with state laws and the customs and practices of Notaries Public.

Most Notaries take an oath of office and/or sign a Notary bond, which even more solemnly bind them to perform their notarial acts competently and faithfully.

The most important obligation a Notary has to the public he serves is to judge what acts constitute the practice of law and what acts constitute the practice of a Notary Public. If the Notary, who is not an attorney, is asked to perform a notarial act that requires the preparation of, or the giving of advice in regard to the preparation of, a legal document or form, the Notary should always obtain the advice of an attorney unless he has had special education and training.

The attorney who notarizes a document after drafting and giving legal advice in connection with the same transaction is faced with the ethically questionable position of assuming the inconsistent dual roles of impartial witness-Notary Public and advocate-attorney.

Many of the states have granted Notaries Public powers or authority to perform acts that constitute the practice of law. Nevertheless, every Notary is firmly bound to make the final judgment: If he is not an attorney or has not been sufficiently educated and trained, he should not attempt to perform the notarial act. If he is an attorney, the dual roles of witness and advocate do present ethical questions.

The Notary should realize that regardless of his authorization and even duty to perform a notarial act, if there is any question in his opinion whether he can competently perform that notarial act, he will be doing himself, as well as his constituent, a favor in asking for legal advice from an attorney.

Mental and Physical Qualifications

It is obvious that every Notary should be capable of reading and writing the English language. The laws of some states require that a Notary applicant be able to read and write, while other states require no evidence that the Notary is physically and mentally capable of performing notarial acts. Nevertheless, the Notary in almost all states does take an oath of office that binds him to perform his duties faithfully, with skill, diligence, integrity and honesty. The Notary who cannot read or write, or whose eyesight has failed beyond the point of being able to identify persons appearing before him or reading the notarial certificate he is signing, is not capable of faithful performance of duty. He is not serving the public and is subjecting himself to possible lawsuits and liability for damages as a result of his improper performance of duty.

The notarization of a document that has been written in a foreign language should only be performed by a Notary who has a thorough understanding of the foreign language in which the document and/or notarial certificate are written.

The Recorder of Public Documents

The Recorder of Public Documents (also called Custodian of Public Documents or Records) is responsible for the preservation and safekeeping of public documents. He is also obligated to furnish to any member of the public certified copies of all public records that he has in his custody, upon receipt of the proper fee. The Recorder generally affixes his official seal and certificate to any certified copy he furnishes, which states that the copy is a true certified copy of the original which he recorded in his office.

The Notary is often the last person to examine the document before it is turned over to the Recorder's Office. It is, therefore, the obligation of the Notary to perform his notarization so that the essential information on his notarial certificate is legible and capable of being photographed. If the Notary has scribbled his signature or if dates or names are carelessly and illegibly written, it may not be possible for the Recorder or anyone else to read the certificate. It is obvious that this kind of notarization would make those concerned question the document, and the Recorder is fully justified in refusing to record a document or Notary's certificate that cannot be read.

It is incumbent on the Notary to print his name, title, jurisdiction, commission expiration date, and address carefully and legibly (preferably with a rubber stamp) under his signature on all documents he notarizes. The requirements on official seals vary from state to state, but regardless of whether or not it is required by law, the

Notary should squeeze his official seal embosser over the letters "L.S." somewhere in a blank space on the notarized document, as explained in the section on official seal embossers.

Some Notaries squeeze the official seal embosser directly over their own signatures or over the person's signature being notarized. There is a question whether this kind of notarization makes the signature (over which the seal embosser has been impressed) illegible. If the signature is illegible, it may be someone else's signature. In a case of suspected forgery, it would be difficult to compare the authentic signature with a signature over which a seal impression had been placed. On the other hand, a signature over which the official seal has been squeezed will be very difficult to forge or copy unless the forger has also obtained a copy of the signature that does not have the seal embosser's impression. In the absence of a directive or law to the contrary, it is probably best to follow the practice of squeezing the seal embosser over the letters "L.S." (as described in the section on official seals), thus preventing, if possible, the indentations from obscuring any writing or printing on the document.

Competence of the Parties

The laws of each state vary widely with respect to the notarization of documents for persons who are incompetent. The Notary should avoid being placed in the position of having to decide whether a person is sufficiently competent to fully understand the agreement he is signing or the oath or affidavit he is taking. The Notary should either seek counsel from his own attorney or advise the party who appears to be incompetent to go to an attorney himself. If a party is declared to have been incompetent at the time the agreement was signed and notarized, the agreement could be declared null and void. If the party is blind,

senile, a minor, or does not seem to understand the importance of the document he is signing, the Notary will do
himself, as well as the party, a service if he asks him to go
to an attorney. Though Notary law may authorize the
Notary to notarize a document for an incompetent person,
the Notary is taking the risk of later having to appear as a
witness if a question arises.

In some states a married woman, by reason of being a
"femme couvert" or "woman under coverture," is required
to acknowledge her signing of a document privately and
apart from her husband. A special form of certificate of
acknowledgment is required and the Notary must be careful to perform his notarial act in accordance with the
terms of the certificate and the Notary laws of his state.

Certificate of Authority

In some cases it is necessary to mail a document out of
state to be notarized in another state or foreign country.
Because of the diversity in Notary law, custom, and practice, each of the states has enacted laws that provide that
"out-of-state" Notaries should (under certain circumstances) obtain what is variously called a Certificate
of Authority, Certificate of Official Character, Certificate
of Authentication, or Certificate of Prothonotary. This
certificate is furnished by the public officer in charge of
keeping the list of all Notaries Public in his jurisdiction.

A typical form of certificate of authority would be as
follows:

I *(Insert county or state officer's name and title)* of the
State of_____, County of_____,
which office (or court) is an office (or court) of record
having a seal, do hereby certify that *(Insert name of
Notary)* by and before whom the foregoing (or annexed) acknowledgment was taken, was at the time of
taking the same a Notary Public residing (or au-

thorized to act) in said county or state, and was authorized by the laws of said state to take and certify acknowledgments in said state, and further, that I am acquainted with his handwriting and that I believe that the signature and official seal to the certificate of acknowledgment are genuine.

In testimony whereof, I have hereunto set my hand and affixed the seal of this office (or court) this _____ day of _____, 19____. *(Officer's signature, followed by his name, title, and jurisdiction printed.)*

The officer's official seal is impressed in the space provided on the certificate.

If a person or office from out of state desires (regardless of whether or not the law so states) a certificate of authority, that person or office will attach a letter to the document requesting that the certificate of authority be obtained after the document has been notarized. Often the Notary will receive a document to be notarized without specific instruction from the out-of-state party on whether a certificate of authority is required. A certificate of authority is rarely required when a Notary is notarizing a document for a party in his own state, which document is to be used or recorded in his own state.

A document that appears to have been notarized properly (with the Notary's signature, printed name, title, jurisdiction, commission expiration date, address under his signature, and an impression of his official seal embosser over the letters "L.S.") is more apt to be accepted and considered valid in an out-of-state office than a document in which some part of the Notary's certificate is illegible or in which there are no indentations made by a seal embosser.

Disqualifying Interest

The Notary's duties are confined to those of an impartial witness as contrasted with those of an advocate or agent. The Notary is appointed as a public officer to perform notarial acts for all citizens in his jurisdiction. He is, therefore, obligated to act as an impartial and unbiased witness. The terms, "customer," or "client," are often used improperly to denote the person for whom the Notary acts as impartial witness. The person for whom notarial acts are performed by a Notary is the Notary's "constituent."

The Notary who acts both as impartial witness and as advocate or agent in connection with the same transaction can be accused, at a later date by a signer who wants to void or rescind the agreement, of unduly influencing and/or coercing the signer. By substantially benefiting financially (in addition to his Notary fee), by drafting or offering advice on how to complete a blank printed legal form, or advocating the signing of a legal document, the Notary puts himself in the inconsistent and questionable dual roles of advocate and impartial witness-Notary. Given time to think over the terms of the agreement, the signer could change his mind, and, wishing to rescind the agreement, make a claim that he signed at a time when he was incompetent, was unduly influenced and even coerced into signing by the Notary who acted both as advocate and impartial witness-Notary.

Occasionally, a Notary may be asked to notarize a document in which he himself is a party to the agreement or a representative of a party to the agreement. If the Notary stands to make a substantial financial gain by notarizing such a document, he should refer it to another Notary and avoid the risk of a lawsuit initiated on the basis of his financial interest in the agreement.

The question of how much is a "substantial" financial gain depends on the specific case and ultimately can only be decided in a court of law. With this in mind, if there is any question, the Notary should refer the party to another Notary, the Notary fee involved not being worth the chance of a lawsuit.

A Notary should never, under any circumstances, notarize his own signature.

QUESTIONS (Chapter 6)

1. What is the difference between the practice of an attorney and the practice of a Notary?

2. Should a Notary write his name or affix his seal over any writing or printing on a document? Why?

3. Why is it important that the Notary's signature as well as all writing on the document and certificate be legible?

4. What is disqualifying interest?

5. Should a Notary provide a notarization if the document and/or certificate are written in a language foreign to the Notary?

6. Should a Notary refuse to notarize a document for a person who doesn't appear to understand the contents of the document? Why?

7. Is it advisable for a Notary who is an attorney or agent for the signer to ask another person to perform notarial acts in connection with the same transaction? Why?

CHAPTER 7

Civil and Criminal Liability

Civil Liability

A Notary being a ministerial officer is liable for his negligence regardless of intention, as distinguished from judicial officers who are liable only for their corrupt and intentional misconduct. Thus the Notary is liable to an injured party for all damages sustained as a result of the Notary's errors, omissions, neglect, improper performance of duty, or misconduct in the performance of his notarial acts. He may be held liable regardless of whether the damages sustained were caused by an intentional act or an unintentional act.

The application for a notarial commission usually contains a statement to be signed by the Notary applicant and his endorsers or references. This statement is generally in the form of a declaration that the applicant is a person of integrity and good moral character who is competent and capable of performing his notarial acts in a skillful and diligent manner.

In addition to the declaration on the application for Notary Public (which is sometimes required to be notarized), the applicant is generally required to take an oath of office that is administered by another Notary or public officer who pledges that he will, without favor or partiality, discharge the duties of Notary Public honestly, faithfully, and diligently.

The Notary Public Bond

Furthermore, many states also require that the Notary Public be bonded. The Notary is required to sign a Notary bond, in which his name is specified as principal. The bonding company and the Notary (as principal) are bound to pay any person who sustains damages as a result of the Notary's improper performance of duty. A typical form of Notary bond signed by the Notary and the bonding company reads as follows:

Know all men by these presents: that we *(Insert Notary's name)* as Principal and *(Insert Insurance Company's name)* are held and firmly bound, unto the State of _____ , in the sum of *(Insert amount of bond),* to be paid to the said State, or its assigns, for which payment well and truly to be made we bind ourselves, our heirs, executors and successors, jointly and severally, firmly by these presents.

Whereas, the above bound principal was appointed a Notary Public in and for the State of _____ , for the term of _____ years commencing on _____ , 19 _____ .

Now therefore, the condition of the above obligation is such that if the said principal shall well, truly and faithfully, perform all the duties of his office that are now, or may hereafter be required, prescribed or defined by law, or by any rule or regulation made under the express or implied authority of any statute and all duties and acts undertaken, assumed, or performed by him by virtue or color of his office, then the above obligation to be void, otherwise to remain in full force and virtue.

The Notary signs as principal and the attorney-in-fact for the bonding company signs as surety. Their signatures are notarized or witnessed.

It is evident that the Notary bond is not an insurance policy. It protects any person (except the Notary and the bonding company) who sustains damages as a result of the Notary's improper performance of duty. The Notary bond is basically a guarantee to the public by the bonding company and the Notary to the effect that the company will reimburse any member of the public who sustains damages as a result of the Notary's improper act. The bonding company may institute proceedings against the Notary to obtain reimbursement from him for all sums the company has paid as a result of his improper performance of duty.

Criminal Liability

The application to become a Notary Public, the oath of office, and the Notary bond all make it very clear that the Notary must be a person who can be depended upon to exercise good judgment in the performance of his duties. The Notary cannot and will not be excused because he did not read his notarial certificate carefully when he signed it. If the certificate states that the person appeared before the Notary and it is later determined that the person did not appear before the Notary (or telephoned the Notary), the Notary is not only liable to the person who sustains damage but he is also liable to criminal prosecution, in that he has signed a false and perhaps fraudulent certificate.

There are certain functions that a Notary Public should not attempt to perform unless he has had special training and education. In some states Notaries are authorized and empowered to solemnize marriages and/or act as justices of the peace and "conservators of the peace." The Notary should realize that although he is authorized by state law to perform a particular notarial act, if he performs that act improperly he may cause another person to suffer substantial losses. He may be held liable to pay damages to all injured parties and also be subject to fines and imprisonment.

The Notary's wrongful act need not be the sole and only cause of the injuries in a claim. He can be held liable even if his improper act was only one of the causes of injuries sustained. The Notary may be held criminally, as well as civilly liable by a party, and cannot avoid the penalties of fines and/or imprisonment on the basis of his ignorance of the law or his statement that "I didn't think it was important."

The impersonation of a Notary, or the continuation in office of a Notary whose commission has expired, is punishable in many states by fines and imprisonment.

Notary Errors and Omissions Insurance

A Notary's Errors and Omissions Insurance Policy is available in some states, which protects the Notary in case he is forced to pay an injured party as a result of his unintentional errors or omissions. This type of coverage will not protect the Notary if he signs a false certificate or if he has not exercised reasonable care and diligence in the performance of his notarial acts.

QUESTIONS (Chapter 7)

1. What is a Notary bond and what is its purpose?

2. What is a Notary errors and omissions insurance policy and how does it protect the Notary?

3. Who is liable to pay for damages resulting from a Notary's errors, omissions, neglect, improper performance of duty, or misconduct in the performance of a notarial act?

4. Can the bonding company demand reimbursement from the Notary if it is required to pay anyone suffering damages caused by the Notary's improper notarial act? Explain.

5. Will a Notary's errors and omissions insurance policy protect a Notary if he notarizes a document for a party who telephoned the Notary to say he signed the document?

6. Would the telephoned acknowledgment described in Question 5 be considered to be a false certificate signed by a Notary?

CHAPTER 8

20th Century Notarial Acts

Computer Signatures and Photocopiers

The laws and statutes for Notaries Public in the 1800's were based on ancient customs and practices as well as on the business needs of the colonial communities. At that time the United States represented a vast area, which today has been diminished by unimagined progress in transportation and communication. Thus it is now possible and necessary for Notaries Public in the United States to adopt practices and procedures that will satisfy the need for notarization in the 20th Century.

The words "known to me," used in the acknowledgment certificate, impose an obligation to properly identify the signer to be the person signing before the Notary and acknowledging to the Notary his intention that the terms contained in the agreement are those intended to be binding and in effect. Notary laws drafted in the late 1800's and early 1900's were not designed to handle a population of two hundred and thirty million people. Impersonation and forgery are relatively simple today, with the help of the computer that prints a person's signature on checks in fractions of a second, together with the machine photocopier that makes facsimiles of a document, including the signature, in color. The Notary Public must use at least reasonable care to make a distinguishing mark on all pages of the document, identify the person appearing before him, and see that the person signs the document and record book or journal in his presence.

To properly identify himself, a person should present to the Notary one or more pieces of evidence containing name, signature, photo, fingerprints and any other information that will assure the Notary that the person is the person he says he is. By retaining the actual signature of the person in his Notary record book or journal, the Notary will have evidence that the document was signed in his presence at the time and place stated in the Notary's record book or journal in case such evidence is ever needed.

The written signature of an individual is no longer the distinctive mark that reveals that party's intent that an act be performed or an agreement be in effect. The signature of an individual may be photocopied in seconds at a cost of a few pennies. The distinctive marks today, which cannot be copied except by expensive machines or computers, are the perforated holes in the computer card, the machine-sensitive ink on a bank check, and the indentations made by the Notary's official seal embosser. Even the signature that appears on many checks and computer cards is machine made and is printed only because it makes the check or computer card look "authentic."

Because the Notary's signature may be easily machine photocopied and because there are still documents that must be preserved as originals and easily distinguished from copies of originals, the Notary is obligated to use an official seal embosser.

Combating Forgery

The ease with which an original document may be

altered and represented to be an original, even when the Notary has used an official seal embosser, obligates the Notary to make and keep a detailed record book or journal of his notarial acts. He must pay particular attention to recording the names of persons whose signatures are notarized, obtaining an example of their signatures in his official record book and recording the kinds of identification presented by those persons whose signatures are notarized.

Recent advances in the technology of copying machines now make it possible to reproduce a machine copy in color. It thus becomes very difficult to distinguish a machine made color copy from the original.

A "correcting" typewriter ribbon has also been made available that permits the typist to remove the ink from the paper when making a correction rather than applying a white substance to correct an error. These miracle inventions have made it easier for the forger. To deter fraudulent reproductions or alterations of this kind, a specially-treated transparent adhesive tape has been manufactured to be applied on critical areas of documents, such as on the certificate of acknowledgment where names are filled in by the Notary. This transparent adhesive tape can be used to cover critical areas on any document, such as the dollar amount line of a check or the description area on a grant deed. The tape tears easily if an attempt is made to remove it. It cannot be easily removed and leaves evidence of its removal (unlike ordinary transparent tape) if it is removed from the document.

In an age of miracle inventions, the Notary Public has greater responsibilities than ever before. Amidst the multitude of Notary laws, many of which were enacted a hundred years ago, and a confusion of customs and practices that have grown out of two thousand years of civilization, the Notary must use sound judgment to perform his notarial act effectively. The modern business community now requires a responsible person, impartial and unbiased, to act as a witness to the signing of important documents. Modern copy machines and computerized signatures have made new standards of practice for all Notaries a necessity. Only with the aid of a competent attorney, a knowledge of the customs and practices of the Notary Public, an understanding of the Notary laws in his own state, and the realization that his notarial act is of prime importance to every individual in this modern society will the Notary perform his duties faithfully and effectively.

QUESTIONS (Chapter 8)

1. Does the signature of an individual carry the same significance today as it did during the Colonial period?

2. Why is it more important today than ever before for the Notary to properly identify the person for whom he performs notarial acts?

3. What evidence can a Notary present at a later date to prove that the signer of the document appeared before him and was properly identified as the person who signed the document?

4. How does a Notary's seal embosser help to prevent forgery?

Grover Cleveland

President of the United States of America,

To all who shall see these Presents, Greeting:

Know Ye, *That, reposing special trust and confidence*

do appoint him to be Notary Public for the District of

fulfill the duties of that Office according to Law, and

privileges, and emoluments thereunto of right appertaining

of five years from the date hereof.

In testimony whereof, *I have caused these Letters to*

hereunto affixed.

Given *under my hand, at the City of Washington, the 3rd*

Lord one thousand eight hundred and eighty-eight ——,

of America the 112th

By the President:

T. F. Bay

in the Integrity and Ability of *Milton C. Barnard*, I

olumbia; and do authorize and empower him to execute and

to have and to hold the said *Office,* with all the powers,

to him, the said *Milton C. Barnard*, for the term

be made *Patent* and the seal of the *United States* to be

day of *January*, in the year of our

and of the *Independence* of the *United States*

Grover Cleveland

Secretary of State.

This notarial appointment signed by Grover Cleveland in 1888 was granted to Milton C. Barnard for the District of Columbia. This 19th Century commission bearing the Presidential seal, underscores the high regard with which Notaries were held in days gone by.

PART II
NOTARY PUBLIC
GLOSSARY

Without Notaries Public a great many of the functions of state government could not continue, and I am fully aware of the even greater part played by Notaries in the private sector.

JOSEPH T. EDGAR
Secretary of State, Maine

Notaries represent one of our most honored offices, for they are responsible for establishing the undisputed identities of signatures, documents and sometimes individuals. Certainly they are bastions of authenticity in our society.

JOHN A. BURNS
Governor, Hawaii

Notaries Public serve a vital function in our American system of government and are to be commended for their professionalism, dedication and interest in serving their fellowman.

JENNINGS RANDOLPH
U.S. Senator, West Virginia

From the earliest days of history, one finds Notaries Public involved in affairs of both business and state.

MIKE O'CALLAGHAN
Governor, Nevada

NOTARY PUBLIC GLOSSARY

The words chosen for this Glossary have been used for over 20 years by the author and staff of the National Notary Association in communicating with representatives from all sectors of business and law in the United States and its territories. The author has also referred to dictionaries, legal, real estate, insurance, banking, securities, title insurance company, escrow and shorthand writing publications and manuals and the Notary laws of the 50 states and territories of the United States.

The purpose here is to give the reader the general meaning of a word or phrase rather than a precise definition and commentary that would be found in a law dictionary. Complicated sentence structures, grammatical references and lengthy comments have been avoided. As a ministerial public officer serving as an impartial witness, the Notary Public does not give legal or business advice and counsel to his constituents. It is necessary that the Notary know *what* a "trust deed" is, but not necessarily *how* it is drawn or whether it is protecting the business interests of any of the parties to the agreement.

This *is* a Glossary not a dictionary. It contains the words used by Notaries Public who are trained and often licensed to serve as advocates or professional consultants and advisors in a position that is not one of a Notary Public. Knowing the meaning of the words given in this Glossary does not replace or substitute for a dictionary, professional manual or many years of study, training and professional practice.

R.C.R.

A

ABSENTEE VOTER'S BALLOT. A ballot used by a voter who is unable to go to his designated voting place because of physical disability, religious reasons, or distance.

ACCEPTANCE. 1. The act of agreeing to an action or offer of another. 2. A term used in connection with negotiable instruments. Consult local area banking authorities.

ACCRUE. To become due; to come by way of increase; to come into existence.

ACKNOWLEDGE. To admit or recognize the existence of an agreement by signing as evidence of one's intention that the agreement shall be binding and in full force and effect. See ACKNOWLEDGMENT, CERTIFICATE OF.

ACKNOWLEDGMENT. 1. The act of admitting or recognizing the existence of an agreement by signing as evidence of one's intention that the agreement shall be binding and in full force and effect. A Notary takes the *acknowledgment* of his constituent. 2. The certificate (usually signed and sealed by a Notary) affixed to the document. See ACKNOWLEDGMENT, CERTIFICATE OF.

ACKNOWLEDGMENT, CERTIFICATE OF. A written statement, affixed to an agreement, signed and sealed by an authorized official (usually a Notary) that states in a form, usually prescribed by law, that the official took the acknowledgment of the person who signed the agreement. See ACKNOWLEDGE, ACKNOWLEDGMENT.

ACKNOWLEDGMENT, CERTIFICATE OF, (CORPORATE FORM). A Notary's certificate that states, in a form usually prescribed by law, that the one who signed the agreement was a titled officer of a corporation.

ACKNOWLEDGMENT, CERTIFICATE OF, (INDIVIDUAL FORM). A Notary's certificate that states, in a form usually prescribed by law, that the document was signed by a person (individual).

ACKNOWLEDGMENT, CERTIFICATE OF, (ON OATH OF A SUBSCRIBING WITNESS). A Notary's certificate that states, in a form usually prescribed by law, that the person who signed the agreement to which the certificate was affixed, did not appear before the Notary, but that the subscribing witness personally known to the Notary took an oath or affirmation before the Notary that the document was signed and acknowledged in the presence of the subscribing witness. Also called a Certificate of Acknowledgment on oath of a credible witness.

ACKNOWLEDGMENT, CERTIFICATE OF, (PARTNERSHIP FORM). A Notary's certificate that states, in a form usually prescribed by law, that the document was signed by a person who is a partner.

ACKNOWLEDGMENT, CERTIFICATE OF, (PARTY PROVEN ON OATH OF SUBSCRIBING WITNESS). A Notary's certificate that states, in a form usually prescribed by law, that the person who signed the agreement to which the certificate was affixed, was satisfactorily proven to be the person, who signed, by a subscribing witness who took an oath or affirmation before the Notary that the signer was known to him to be the person who acknowledged signing the document. Also called a Certificate of Acknowledgment, party proven on oath of a credible witness, Party Proven and Certificate of Proof.

ACKNOWLEDGMENT, CERTIFICATE OF, (SIGNATURE BY MARK). A Notary's certificate that states, in a form usually prescribed by law, that the person whose acknowledgment was taken, was unable to sign his name and at his request, his name was written near the place where he made his mark and the place where the witnesses had signed.

ADJUDGE. To decide, rule upon or give a judicial decision.

ADJUDICATION. A judicial decision, sentence, or decree.

ADMINISTER. 1. To give ritually, as, administer an oath. 2. To oversee or manage.

ADMINISTRATOR. 1. A party chosen by the court to handle the estate of a person. 2. One who manages or oversees.

ADULT. A person who, by law, is considered competent by virtue of his attained age. Also called lawful age, legal age and majority. Consult local area legal counsel. See MINOR.

ADVOCATE. 1. To support or argue in favor of a cause. 2. An attorney-at-law.

AFFIANT. The person who takes an oath or affirmation. The person to whom an oath or affirmation is administered. Sometimes called a deponent. See AFFIDAVIT.

AFFIDAVIT. A document that contains a statement, made under oath or affirmation, signed by the affiant and a jurat (certificate) signed and sealed by a Notary. See DEPOSITION.

AFFIDAVIT OF AUTHENTICITY. 1. An affidavit in which the affiant states that he has compared a document to which the affidavit is attached with another purported to be the original and found it to be a true and correct copy of the original. See CERTIFIED COPY. 2. An affidavit in which the affiant states that he has examined an object (such as an antique) and in his capacity as an expert has found it to be genuine.

AFFIDAVIT OF BIRTH. An affidavit in which the affiant states that he has personal knowledge of the date and place of birth of another and the source of such knowledge.

AFFIDAVIT OF DEATH OF JOINT TENANT. An affidavit in which the affiant who is the surviving joint tenant states that another joint tenant is deceased. A certified copy of the death certificate is attached. Consult local area legal counsel.

AFFIDAVIT OF REGISTRATION. An affidavit in which the affiant, who is unable to appear before a Deputy Registrar of Voters, makes the statements necessary to qualify to vote under oath before another official such as a Notary.

AFFIRM. See AFFIRMATION.

AFFIRMATION. A solemn statement, equivalent by law to an oath, but without religious significance or reference to a Supreme Being.

AFFIX. To attach, add to, or impress.

AGENT. One who performs acts for, or does business as an intermediary for another called a principal. See BROKER.

AGGREGATE. 1. The entire amount. 2. Considered collectively as a whole.

AGREEMENT. An understanding (often put in writing and signed) by two or more people.

ALIEN. 1. A foreigner; a person who is not a citizen of the United States. 2. Foreign.

ALTERATION. A change or amendment.

AMENDMENT. A change, correction or alteration.

APPEAL. Action by a defeated party in a lawsuit to have a judgment reversed.

APPEARANCE. The physical presence of another person in the view of the Notary.

APPOINTMENT. A document in which a superior officer designates and/or confers title, powers, responsibility and authority to another. A notarial appointment. See LICENSE.

ASQDE. AMERICAN SOCIETY OF QUESTIONED DOCUMENTS EXAMINERS. A group of individuals who are experts in the field of analyzing the writings and markings on documents primarily to detect or avoid counterfeits.

ASSIGN. To transfer property, title, or ownership.

ATTEST. 1. To indicate genuineness by signing as a witness. 2. To sign as a witness.

ATTESTATION. See ATTEST.

ATTESTED COPY. See CERTIFIED COPY.

ATTORNEY-AT-LAW. A person who has had specialized education and training in connection with the law profession and is licensed after passing an examination to perform those acts which constitute the practice of law. Titles such as advocate, counsellor, solicitor, proctor, attorney, counsel, lawyer, legal counsel, and esquire, are also used to identify an attorney-at-law.

ATTORNEY-IN-FACT. See POWER OF ATTORNEY.

AUTHENTIC. Genuine, not counterfeit.

AUTHENTICATE. To make authentic.

AUTHENTICATION. A statement relating to genuineness. See CERTIFICATE OF AUTHORITY, CERTIFIED COPY.

AUTHENTICATION, CERTIFICATE OF. See CERTIFICATE OF AUTHORITY, CERTIFIED COPY.

AUTHORITY, CERTIFICATE OF. See CERTIFICATE OF AUTHORITY.

B

BEARER. The person in possession of a negotiable instrument. Also called the Holder.

BENEFICIAL INTEREST. A profit, benefit, advantage, right, title, cash or property that accrues or may accrue. (Definition varies depending upon each case considered by the court.)

BENEFICIARY. Anyone who receives or is designated to receive profits, benefit, advantage, right, title, interest, cash, or property.

BILL OF EXCHANGE. A written order to pay a specified sum of money. Also called a draft. Consult local area banking authorities.

BIRTH AFFIDAVIT. See AFFIDAVIT OF BIRTH.

BLANKS (IN A DOCUMENT). Spaces in a document or certificate that can be filled in to complete or clarify the writing.

BONA FIDE. Latin. "Good faith." In or with good faith; sincere.

BOND. See SURETY BOND, NOTARY BOND.

BOROUGH. An area within a state whose boundaries are determined by political and population considerations. See COUNTY, PARISH.

BOTTOMRY. A contract whereby a ship's owner obtains a loan by pledging the ship as security. If the ship is lost, the owner is not liable for payment, and the lender loses his money. Consult local area legal counsel and maritime authorities.

BREACH OF CONTRACT. Failure to carry out the terms of an agreement.

BROKER. One who performs acts for, or does business as an agent or intermediary for another called a principal.

C

CANCEL. To strike out, destroy, or make void.

CAPTION. A number, descriptive heading or title used to identify and classify a document for filing purposes.

CERTIFICATE. A written statement, signed by an official, describing acts performed in his official capacity. See NOTARIAL CERTIFICATE.

CERTIFICATE OF ACKNOWLEDGMENT. See ACKNOWLEDG-
MENT, CERTIFICATE OF.

CERTIFICATE OF AUTHORITY. A certificate, signed and sealed by
an official or his representative who appointed the Notary, attached to a notarized document. It states that the Notary's signature and seal are authentic and the Notary is qualified to perform
notarial acts. Also called a Certificate of Official Character, Certificate of Authentication, Certificate of Prothonotary, and Certificate of Magistracy.

CERTIFICATE OF MAGISTRACY. See CERTIFICATE OF AUTHOR-
ITY.

CERTIFIED COPY. A copy of a document and certificate signed
and sealed by an official who retains a copy of the original in his
files. The certificate states that the copy is genuine and a true copy
of the document (retained by the official) it purports to represent.
Also known as an Attested Copy. See AFFIDAVIT OF AUTHEN-
TICITY.

CERTIFIED TRANSLATION. A translation to which the certificate
of a translator has been affixed stating that the translation is
genuine and correct. See INTERPRETER.

CERTIFY. To make a statement.

CHATTEL MORTGAGE. A document used in connection with a
mortgage of personal property. Consult local area legal counsel
and banking authorities.

CITIZEN, UNITED STATES. A person born or naturalized in the
United States.

CIVIL ACTION. A lawsuit that has for its object the protection of
private (not public) rights and compensation for their violation.
Not criminal action.

CIVIL LIABILITY. The obligation and responsibility to indemnify
another person for damages caused by improper performance of
duties and acts.

CLAIM. 1. To make a demand or request. 2. A right or interest in
property.

CLAIMANT. The maker of a claim.

CLIENT. The person who employs and pays for professional services and/or advice. See CONSTITUENT.

CODE. A set of specific regulations relating to one particular subject, as criminal code, penal code, government code, civil code.

CODICIL. An amendment, or addition to a will.

COERCE. To force or threaten another to do something against his will.

COGNOMEN. Last name, family name, or surname.

COLLATERAL. Property that is pledged to another to guarantee payment of a debt. Consult local area banking authorities.

COLLUSION. A secret understanding made, between two or more people, for the purpose of deceiving another.

COMMERCIAL PAPER. A document whose purpose is to transfer money such as a check, draft or bill of exchange. Also called a negotiable instrument. Consult local area banking authorities.

COMMISSION. 1. Authorization granted by the appropriate state authority to exercise the functions and duties of a Notary. 2. A document that describes the Notary's appointment and term of office, usually issued by the state's officer responsible for appointing Notaries. See APPOINTMENT. 3. Remuneration for services, usually on a percentage basis.

COMMISSIONER OF DEEDS. An official, rarely appointed today, residing outside his home state, appointed and empowered to perform notarial acts for residents of his home state who are temporarily living away from their home state.

COMMON LAW. In the United States, the unwritten law based on customs and precedents set in early English law. Also known as unwritten law.

COMMUNITY PROPERTY. Property acquired while married. Consult local area legal counsel.

COMPETENT. 1. Having the ability to capably act and think. 2. Legally qualified. See INCOMPETENT.

CONFLICTING INTEREST. An interest in a transaction, in which the same person is considered to have opposing opinions or interests.

CONFORM. To make the same, to make a similar copy, that is not represented to be the original. Signatures of the parties may be typed in the space where the signature appears on the original. See /S/.

CONSANGUINITY. Descent from the same ancestor. Blood relationship.

CONSIDERATION. Something of value offered to another in return for an act or promise.

CONSTITUENT. Any person who has the right to demand and receive services from, or to be represented by, an appointed or elected public official. Not a client or a customer.

CONTRACT. A written or oral agreement.

CONVEYANCE. Transfer of title or ownership.

CONVICTION. The judicial act of finding a person guilty.

COPY. 1. To reproduce an original. 2. A duplicate or facsimile.

COPYRIGHT. A document issued by the U.S. Copyright Office, granting to the recipient the exclusive right to print, reprint, copy, translate, dramatize, convert, arrange, adapt, complete, execute, finish, deliver in public, perform and transcribe an original work in the United States.

CORPORATION. A legal entity created by a written agreement for business purposes. Consult local area legal counsel.

COUNTER. Against.

COUNTERFEIT. 1. To make an imitation or copy for the purpose of illegal misrepresentation. 2. A forgery.

COUNTERSIGNATURE. The signature of a person with an official title necessary to authenticate or validate a document.

COUNTY. An area within a state whose boundaries are determined by political and population considerations. See BOROUGH, PARISH.

COUNTY CLERK. A public officer who keeps records and accounts.

COUNTY RECORDER. See RECORDER OF PUBLIC DOCUMENTS.

CREDIBLE. 1. Believable. 2. An honest person of good character and reputation. See ACKNOWLEDGMENT, CERTIFICATE OF (ON

OATH OF SUBSCRIBING WITNESS).

CREDITOR. One who lends money. A lender.

CRIME. A misdemeanor or a felony. A violation of the law that is punishable by fine or imprisonment upon conviction.

CRIMINAL ACTION. A court proceeding that has for its object the conviction and punishment of individuals who commit crimes. Not civil action.

CRIMINAL LIABILITY. The obligation and responsibility a public official has to perform faithfully the duties of his office in conformance to the law with the knowledge that failure to so perform, could be a crime, punishable under the law.

CUSTODIAN OF PUBLIC DOCUMENTS (RECORDS). See RECORDER OF PUBLIC DOCUMENTS.

CUSTOM. An action or procedure repeated over a long period of time and therefore accepted by society.

CUSTOMER. A person who purchases goods or services. See CLIENT, CONSTITUENT.

D

DAMAGE. An injury to person, property or reputation caused by an accident, wrongful act, negligence or omission.

DAMAGES. Money awarded by a court to compensate for damage.

DEBTOR. One who owes money. A borrower.

DECLARATION. A formal statement usually prepared in advance.

DECLARATION OF HOMESTEAD. See HOMESTEAD.

DECLARATION UNDER PENALTY OF PERJURY. A signed statement which, if false, can result in punishment for perjury.

DEED. A document that transfers title to property. See GRANT DEED, QUITCLAIM DEED, TRUST DEED, WARRANTY DEED.

DEFAULT. Failure to act, perform or pay a debt as previously promised or agreed.

DEFENDANT. The party against whom a lawsuit is directed. See PLAINTIFF.

DEFRAUD. To unlawfully trick or deceive.

DEMAND. To claim or require, as to demand payment.

DEPONENT. A person who gives testimony in connection with a deposition under oath or affirmation. Sometimes called the affiant. See AFFIDAVIT, DEPOSITION.

DEPOSE. To give testimony under oath or affirmation in connection with an affidavit or deposition.

DEPOSITION. A document to be used as testimony in a court proceeding, that contains questions and answers given by the deponent (also called an affiant) under oath or affirmation. See AFFIDAVIT.

DISHONOR. See NOTICE OF DISHONOR.

DISQUALIFYING INTEREST. An interest held by a Notary in connection with a transaction that renders him incapable of performing a notarial act as an impartial and unbiased witness. See BENEFICIAL INTEREST, CONFLICTING INTEREST, INCONSISTENT INTEREST.

DISSOLUTION. The ending or breaking up of legal relationships such as partnerships, corporations and marriages.

DOCUMENT. A paper on which writing or printing appears in a legal form, agreement or contract. Also called an instrument.

DOE, JOHN. A person whose name is unknown.

DOWER. The rights of a widow to her husband's property. Consult local area legal counsel.

DRAFT. A written order to pay a specified sum of money. Also called a bill of exchange. Consult local area banking authorities.

DULY QUALIFIED. A person who is deemed capable of performing acts in accordance with the law.

DUPLICATE. 1. A copy of a document that is made to look like the original. A facsimile. 2. To make a copy.

DURESS. Compulsion, coercion or threat of injury to force compliance.

DUTY. Obligation to perform an act or acts.

E

EASEMENT. A right, interest or privilege to use another's property. Consult local area real estate authorities.

EMBOSS. To make indentations and raised areas on paper. See SEAL, EMBOSSER SEAL, NOTARY SEAL, EMBOSSMENT.

EMBOSSER SEAL. 1. A plier-like device that, when squeezed together with paper between the jaws that contain male and female dies, makes indentations and raised areas (called embossments) on paper in the form of a seal. 2. The embossment made by the embosser seal. See SEAL.

EMBOSSMENT. Indentations and raised areas made in paper. See EMBOSSER SEAL, SEAL.

EMINENT DOMAIN. The right of a governing body to take property provided it fairly compensates the owner. Consult local area real estate authorities.

ENCUMBER. To mortgage, lien, give easements, or place restrictions on land or otherwise allow others rights or privileges to real estate. Consult local area real estate authorities.

EMOLUMENT. Compensation. Archaic term. Consult local area legal counsel.

ENDORSE. 1. To express approval. 2. To write on or sign the back of a negotiable instrument such as a check.

ENDORSEE. The one that the endorsor designates to receive payment in connection with an endorsement.

ENDORSEMENT. 1. An expression of approval or recognition given in writing to acknowledge or assure others that a person is qualified to perform certain acts. 2. The endorsor's signature and/or writing usually on the back of a check or negotiable instrument.

ENDORSEMENT GUARANTEED. A phrase stamped on a check signed by a bank officer stating that the signature of the person to whom the check is payable on the back of the check is that person's true signature. Consult local area banking authorities and securities and exchange commission. See SIGNATURE GUARANTEED.

ENDORSOR. The one who signs or writes usually on the back of a check or negotiable instrument.

ENTITY. One or more persons or a thing that has been given a title so that it will be recognized as a body capable of making agreements.

ERASURE. An obliteration. The removal of written matter by rubbing, usually with a piece of rubber.

ERROR. A mistake. See NOTARY ERRORS AND OMISSIONS.

ESCROW. Funds and/or documents conditionally entrusted to an impartial third party with instructions. Consult local area escrow authorities.

ESTATE. 1. Property. 2. An interest in property. Consult local area legal counsel.

EVIDENCE. Something submitted to a court as proof.

EXECUTE. 1. To sign one's name. 2. To perform, complete or accomplish.

EXECUTOR. A man named in the testator's will to manage and settle the estate.

EXECUTRIX. A woman named in the testator's will to manage and settle the estate.

EXEMPLARY DAMAGES. Money awarded in excess of the sum necessary to compensate for the injury inflicted. Punitive or vindictive damages.

EXEMPLIFY. To make a certified copy.

EX OFFICIO. Latin. "By virtue of the office." One who holds an additional title and office automatically. In some states a justice of the peace is a Notary ex officio.

EXPIRATION. The end of something. Termination.

EXTRAORDINARY CARE. The next higher level of care above reasonable care; extreme diligence. See REASONABLE CARE.

F

FACSIMILE. An exact copy or reproduction.

FAIR AND JUST. Qualities, rights, privileges, principles or laws considered acceptable, reasonable and morally right.

FAITHFUL PERFORMANCE. The degree of care and diligence

necessary to capably and competently perform the duties and accept the responsibilities of an office such as that of a Notary.

FALSE. 1. Untrue; not genuine. 2. Misleading and deceitful.

FALSE PRETENSES. Untrue statements and intentional misrepresentations made for the purpose of obtaining something.

FALSE REPRESENTATION. That which is intentionally false and misleading. See MISREPRESENTATION.

FEASANCE. The performance of an act. See MALFEASANCE, MISFEASANCE, NONFEASANCE.

FEDERAL ADVISORY COMMITTEE ON FALSE IDENTIFICATION. A committee composed of 75 volunteers representing 50 federal, state, and local agencies, the commercial sector and the public, established by the United States Attorney General for the purpose of studying the criminal use of false identification and recommending steps, consistent with privacy rights, to combat it. The Committee's report was published in the Federal Register on June 16, 1976.

FEE SIMPLE. Ownership of property. Consult local area escrow and title insurance authorities.

FELONY. A crime more serious than a misdemeanor.

FEMME COUVERT. French. "Married woman." Relates to the legal rights of married women. Consult local area legal counsel.

FICTITIOUS. Imaginary, non-existent.

FIDUCIARY. One who is responsible to manage or administer the funds and/or affairs of another. Consult local escrow, insurance, legal and banking authorities.

FILE. 1. To deliver a document to the proper official for recording. 2. A place where documents are identified, classified and stored.

FINANCIAL INTEREST. A profit, benefit, right, title, cash or property that accrues or may accrue to one. (Definition varies depending upon each case considered by the court).

FINE. A monetary penalty in punishment for a crime.

FOLIO. A unit or division of a document composed of 100 words.

FOREIGN. 1. Concerning another country. 2. Concerning another state.

FOREIGN BILL OF EXCHANGE. A bill of exchange payable outside of the state where it is drawn. Consult local banking authorities. See INLAND BILL OF EXCHANGE.

FORFEIT. 1. To lose the right to something because of error or wrongdoing. 2. A penalty.

FORFEITURE. The loss of a right or deposit because of error or wrongdoing.

FORGE. To fraudulently alter or duplicate the writing on a document.

FORM. A document with blanks to be filled in according to the specific parties and conditions applicable.

FORTHWITH. Immediately; within a reasonable time.

FRAUD. Intentional misrepresentation which when acted upon can cause damage or injury.

FRAUDS, STATUTE OF. Laws that describe the types of contracts and transactions that must be in writing to be enforced.

FRAUDULENT. See FRAUD.

FREE ACT AND DEED. An act done voluntarily.

FREEHOLDER. A person who has title to property.

G

GARNISHMENT. 1. A notice regarding property that has been attached. 2. Withholding a debtor's wages to pay a creditor. Consult local area legal counsel.

GENERAL DAMAGES. See DAMAGES.

GENERAL PARTNERSHIP. See PARTNERSHIP.

GOOD FAITH. Honestly and fairly.

GRANT. 1. The transfer of title or rights to property or the giving of a right or privilege from the grantor to the grantee. 2. To transfer or hand over.

GRANT DEED. A document that transfers title to property from the grantor to another called the grantee. See DEED, QUITCLAIM DEED, WARRANTY DEED.

GRANTEE. The receiver of a grant. See GRANT DEED.

GRANTOR. The one who makes a grant. See GRANT DEED.

GREAT SEAL. The seal of the United States or the seal of an individual state within the United States.

GROSS NEGLIGENCE. A high degree of negligence.

GUARANTEE. The one who accepts the guaranty of the guarantor. See SIGNATURE GUARANTEED, ENDORSEMENT GUARANTEED.

GUARANTOR. The one who gives a guaranty to the guarantee. See GUARANTY.

GUARANTY. An agreement to assume an obligation or perform a service if previous promises are not kept.

GUILTY. Responsible for a delinquency, crime, sin, or wrongdoing.

H

HANDWRITING. The form, style, and character of a person's writing, including the slant of the letters, spacing, and other features that distinguish it from the handwriting of others.

HANDWRITING EXPERT. A person trained to analyze handwriting. See ASQDE.

HEREDITAMENT. Property that can be inherited. See INHERIT.

HOLOGRAPHIC WILL. A will entirely in the handwriting of the testator. Consult local area legal counsel. Also known as Olographic Will. See TESTATOR.

HOMESTEAD. A legal form signed by the owner to exempt property used as a home from forced sale to settle a judgment. Also called a Declaration of Homestead.

HYPOTHECATE. To give as security without giving up title or possession. Consult local area banking authorities and maritime authorities. See BOTTOMRY.

I

IDENTIFICATION. Something used to prove identity such as a driver's license or a passport. See IDENTITY, IDENTIFY.

IDENTIFY. To establish identity; to determine that someone is the person he claims to be. See IDENTIFICATION, IDENTITY.

IDENTITY. The physical characteristics, qualifications, and attributes that distinguish one person from another. See IDENTIFICATION, IDENTIFY.

ILLEGAL. Forbidden by law.

ILLEGIBLE. Unreadable. Not distinct to the eye. Not legible.

IMMIGRANT. A person who immigrates.

IMMIGRATE. To establish residence in a foreign country. See IMMIGRANT, IMMIGRATION.

IMMIGRATION. The act of immigrating. See IMMIGRATE and IMMIGRANT.

IMMUTABLE. Unchangeable.

IMPARTIAL WITNESS. A witness who does not take a side in an argument or discussion. Not an advocate. One who is neutral, unprejudiced and unbiased.

IMPEACH. To accuse of a crime or misconduct.

IMPERSONATE. To act like and/or make oneself look like another person.

IMPOSTOR (IMPOSTER). Intentional misrepresentation by acting like or making oneself look like another, which when acted upon can cause damage or injury.

IMPRESSION. 1. A mark. A photographically reproducible imprint on paper made with a rubber stamp. See RUBBER STAMP SEAL, SEAL. 2. An embossment. Indentations or raised areas made on paper with an embosser. See EMBOSSER SEAL, SEAL.

INCOMPETENCY. The state of being incompetent. See COMPETENT.

INCOMPETENT. 1. A person who is incapable of satisfactorily acting and thinking. 2. Not legally qualified. See COMPETENT.

INCONSISTENT INTEREST. A disqualifying interest in a transaction in which the Notary acts as an advocate or agent and an impartial witness.

INDEMNIFY. To offer or agree to compensate another in case of the occurrence of an event. See NOTARY BOND, SURETY BOND.

INDEMNITY. Compensations promised, offered or given to reimburse another for damages suffered. See NOTARY BOND, SURETY BOND.

INDICTMENT. A formal document in which a jury accuses a person or persons of committing a crime.

INDORSE. See ENDORSE.

INFRACTION. A violation of an agreement, contract, or law.

INHERIT. To receive right or title upon the death of an ancestor. See HERIDITAMENT.

INITIATIVE. A voter's lawful right to join with a specified number of other voters in signing a petition to put proposed legislation on the ballot.

INJUNCTION. A court order that requires the person or entity served to do, not do or stop doing something.

INJUSTICE. That which is unfair, unjust and wrongful. See FAIR AND JUST.

INLAND BILL OF EXCHANGE. A bill of exchange that is payable within the state where it is drawn. Consult local banking authorities. See FOREIGN BILL OF EXCHANGE.

INSTRUMENT. 1. A paper on which writing or printing appears in a legal form, agreement or contract. Also called a document. 2. A device.

INSURANCE, NOTARY ERRORS AND OMISSIONS INSURANCE. See NOTARY ERRORS AND OMISSIONS INSURANCE.

INSURANCE POLICY. An agreement (contract) in which the insurance company (the insuror) agrees to indemnify another (the insured) in case of the occurrence of an event. See NOTARY ERRORS AND OMISSIONS INSURANCE.

INSURED. The person or entity who is to be indemnified in case of the occurrence of an event. See INSURANCE POLICY.

INSURER; INSUROR. The entity, usually an insurance company, who agrees to pay or to indemnify the insured. See INSURANCE POLICY.

INTEGRITY, MORAL. See MORAL INTEGRITY.

INTENT; INTENTION. A person's purpose and state of mind at any one time.

INTEREST. 1. An advantage or right in connection with an agreement or title to property. 2. Money charged for the privilege of using money.

INTERLINEATION. 1. Writing between the lines. 2. Insertion of writing on a document.

INTERPRET. 1. To explain the meaning. 2. To translate that which is written or spoken from one language into another. See TRANSLATION.

INTERPRETATION. 1. An explanation. 2. A translation.

INTERPRETER. A person who translates from one language into another. See TRANSLATION, CERTIFIED TRANSLATION.

INTERROGATORIES. Questions asked by one party in behalf of another, in connection with a court proceeding or inquiry, the answers to which are made under oath or affirmation.

INTESTATE. To die without leaving a will.

INVALID. Not valid. Void.

INVOLUNTARY. 1. Performed without choice, unintentionally by reflex. 2. Performed under compulsion or duress.

IPSO FACTO. Latin. "By the fact itself." As a consequence of the fact or act. Consult local area legal counsel.

IRREGULAR. Done improperly or not according to rules, laws, or customs.

IRRELEVANT. Unrelated; inapplicable. Not pertinent.

J

JOINT TENANCY. The ownership of property by two or more persons in an agreement which, by law, transfers ownership to the survivor(s) upon the death of one of the owners. See TENANCY IN COMMON, COMMUNITY PROPERTY, AFFIDAVIT OF DEATH OF JOINT TENANT. Consult local area legal counsel.

JOURNAL. A book that contains a chronological list of facts, events or transactions.

JOURNAL OF NOTARIAL ACTS. A bound book kept by a Notary, that provides space and titled columns for the constituents' signature and for chronologically recording pertinent data in connection with each notarial act. Also called a Notary Record Book and Notary's Register.

JUDGMENT. 1. The ability to understand, reason and form an opinion. 2. A formal decision or determination made by a court or judge.

JUDICIAL. A general term relating to a court, judge, or the system and administration of justice. Consult local area legal counsel.

JURAT. Latin. "To swear." The certificate, "Subscribed and sworn to before me this ____ day of _____ 19___ ", signed and sealed by the Notary, affixed below the sworn or affirmed statement and signature of the affiant. See AFFIDAVIT.

JURISDICTION. 1. A specified area in which official acts may be performed. 2. The power and authority of a judge to interpret and apply laws in a specified area.

JUST. That which is not unjust. See FAIR AND JUST.

JUSTICE OF THE PEACE. A public officer with powers and jurisdiction specified in state law.

K

KNOW ALL MEN BY THESE PRESENTS. A formal phrase used at the beginning of an agreement near the title meaning that the text of the agreement follows.

KNOWN TO ME TO BE. Also appears as "personally known to me to be" in a certificate of acknowledgment. To recognize and to be familiar with. A ruling is necessary on each case in question. What constitutes sufficient vision to "recognize" and what identification (if any) is sufficient for a Notary to testify to "familiarity" are the questions subject to definition and interpretation by the court. See IDENTIFICATION.

L

LAST WILL AND TESTAMENT. See WILL.

LAWFUL. Legal. Authorized by law. Not forbidden by law.

LAWFUL AGE. Legal age. See ADULT, MINOR.

LAWSUIT. An action or proceeding in a court.

LAWYER. An attorney. See ATTORNEY-AT-LAW.

LEASE. 1. An agreement conveying rights to property from the lessor to the lessee in return for rent. 2. The act of making such an agreement. Consult local area legal counsel.

LEGAL. 1. In accordance with the forms and usages of law. 2. Pertaining to law.

LEGAL ADVICE. Advice concerning the law given by a lawyer. See ATTORNEY-AT-LAW.

LEGAL AGE. Lawful age. See ADULT, MINOR.

LEGAL COUNSEL. A lawyer. See ATTORNEY-AT-LAW.

LEGAL ENTITY. One or more persons or a thing that has been given a title so that it will be recognized as a body capable of making legal agreements.

LEGIBLE. Readable. Distinct to the eye; not illegible.

LEGISLATURE. The lawmaking body of a government.

LESSEE. The legal entity who leases property and pays rent to the lessor. See LEASE.

LESSOR. The legal entity who leases property and receives rent from the lessee. See LEASE.

LET. To lease.

LETTER OF ATTORNEY. See POWER OF ATTORNEY.

LIABILITY. A duty, debt, obligation or responsibility.

LIABLE. Obliged, bound or responsible.

LICENSE. A document in which an officer or authority allows or grants specified rights to the bearer. See APPOINTMENT.

LIEN. A right, claim or encumbrance on property. See MECHANICS LIEN.

LIMITATIONS, STATUTE OF. A law indicating the time beyond which legal action cannot be initiated. Consult local area legal counsel.

LIMITED PARTNERSHIP. See PARTNERSHIP.

LIS PENDENS. Latin. "A pending lawsuit." Consult local area legal counsel.

LITIGANT. The plaintiff or defendant in a lawsuit.

LITIGATION. A court action. A lawsuit.

LIVING WILL. See RIGHT TO DIE DECLARATION.

LOCUS SIGILLI. Latin. "The location where the seal is placed." Abbreviated *L.S.*, the letters are printed or written at the place over which the Notary's seal embossment is placed. The misalignment of the paper and letters "L.S." caused by the embosser helps one distinguish an original from an altered facsimile that does not have the same embossment.

LOYALTY OATH. An oath to the effect that the affiant has neither allegiance to nor sympathy for governments and institutions believed to be hostile to the United States.

L.S. See LOCUS SIGILLI.

M

MAJORITY. See ADULT.

MALFEASANCE. Unlawful performance of an act. See FEASANCE, MISFEASANCE, NONFEASANCE.

MALPRACTICE. The improper performance of an act that causes damage.

MANDATE. 1. To command. 2. An authoritative charge or command.

MARITIME LAW. Rules, laws and decisions pertaining to navigation and commerce on large bodies of water.

MARITIME PROTEST. A statement by a ship's captain that damages to his ship were caused by storms or other forces beyond his control, and were not due to negligence or misconduct. Also called a Marine Protest. Consult local area maritime authorities.

MECHANICS LIEN. A claim or right that establishes a lien on property, made by a workman or supplier who has not been paid for services or supplies delivered to the property. Consult local area legal counsel.

MERCANTILE LAW. The law pertaining to business and trade.

Also called commercial law, law merchant and custom of merchants.

MINISTERIAL ACTS. Acts performed without the exercise of judgment or discretion, but in accordance with explicit instructions or rules·

MINOR. A person who, by law, is not old enough to be considered competent because of his age. Consult local area legal counsel. See ADULT.

MISCONDUCT. An intentionally wrongful, unlawful, forbidden or improper act.

MISDEMEANOR. A lesser crime than a felony.

MISFEASANCE. Improper or wrongful performance of an act. See FEASANCE, MALFEASANCE, NONFEASANCE.

MISNOMER. An error in name; the use of a wrong name for a party to a document or court proceeding.

MISREPRESENTATION. That which is intentionally *or* unintentionally false and misleading. See FALSE REPRESENTATION.

MISSTATEMENT. An incorrect statement.

MISTAKE. An error; a misunderstanding of meaning or intent.

MORAL INTEGRITY. Conditions or qualities of character and reputation considered necessary for an individual to competently perform specified acts or hold office.

MORAL TURPITUDE. Conditions or qualities of character or actions that are considered vile, base, wrong, immoral or improper.

MORTGAGE. A legal form that permits a borrower (the mortgagor) to retain control of property by transfering the title to another (the mortgagee or lender) during the time the loan is outstanding. In the event the borrower defaults, the mortgagee will acquire possession of the property as well as the title. Consult local area real estate and banking authorities.

MORTGAGEE. The lender. See MORTGAGE.

MORTGAGOR. The borrower. See MORTGAGE.

MUNIMENTS. Documents that can be used as evidence to prove title to real property. Consult local area legal counsel and title insurance officials.

N

NATIONAL NOTARY ASSOCIATION. A professional, educational organization formed in 1957 for the purpose of helping Notaries Public to learn recommended ethical practices and procedures so as to better serve the public interest. Headquartered in Woodland Hills, California.

NATIVE. A person born in the country of which he is a citizen.

NE VARIETUR. Latin. "It must not be altered." A term used to identify a document. Consult local area legal counsel.

NEGLECT. To disregard; to fail to do something that should be done; to fail to exercise care in doing something.

NEGLIGENCE. Carelessness. The lack of ordinary or reasonable care. Negligence is not intentional.

NEGOTIABLE. Transferrable. See NEGOTIABLE INSTRUMENT.

NEGOTIABLE INSTRUMENT. A document whose purpose is to transfer money such as a check, draft or bill of exchange. Also called commercial paper. Consult local area banking authorities.

NOLO CONTENDERE. Latin. "I do not wish to contest it." A plea made by a defendant accused of a crime, almost equivalent to a plea of "guilty." Consult local area legal counsel.

NONACCEPTANCE. Refusal to pay as directed on a negotiable instrument. Consult local area banking authorities.

NONFEASANCE. Omission. Failure to perform an act that should be done. See FEASANCE, MALFEASANCE, NONFEASANCE.

NONPAYMENT. Failure to pay a debt when due.

NONRESIDENCE. Residence outside a particular jurisdiction.

NONRESIDENT. A person who lives outside a particular jurisdiction.

NOTARIAL ACT. An act performed in conformance with the Notary law by a qualified and commissioned Notary Public. A notarization.

NOTARIAL CERTIFICATE. A written statement, signed and sealed by a Notary, describing a notarial act. Also called a Notary Certificate.

NOTARIAN®. A Notary, certified by the National Notary Association, who has passed a written examination and committed himself to uphold and maintain ethical and procedural standards in accordance with the Rules of Notarial Practice. See RULES OF NOTARIAL PRACTICE.

NOTARIUS. In early Roman times, a person who wrote for people who had not learned to write.

NOTARIZATION. An act performed in conformance with the Notary law by a qualified and commissioned Notary Public. A notarial act.

NOTARIZE. To perform a notarial act or notarization.

NOTARY. See NOTARY PUBLIC.

NOTARY-AT-LARGE. A Notary with statewide jurisdiction.

NOTARY BOND. An agreement called a bond signed by a surety company and a Notary (called the principal) in which the surety company agrees to indemnify anyone who suffers damages caused by the Notary's improper performance of notarial acts, providing the Notary himself cannot pay the damages.

NOTARY CERTIFICATE. A written statement, signed and sealed by a Notary, describing a notarial act. Also called a notarial certificate.

NOTARY ERRORS AND OMISSIONS INSURANCE. An insurance policy that obligates the insurance company (insuror) to pay damages and for legal counsel to defend a Notary accused of error or omission, in connection with the performance of a notarial act. Consult local area insurance authorities.

NOTARY PUBLIC. Also called a Notary. A person appointed by a state official to serve the public as a disinterested witness, to take acknowledgments, administer oaths and affirmations and to perform such other acts as are allowed or required by law.

NOTARY RECORD BOOK. See JOURNAL OF NOTARIAL ACTS.

NOTARY SEAL. 1. The imprint or embossment made by the seal of a Notary. 2. A device used by a notary that makes an imprint or embossment. See EMBOSSER SEAL, RUBBER STAMP SEAL, SEAL.

NOTARY TAPE #819. A pressure-sensitive transparent adhesive

tape, specially treated to resist removal after it is applied over un-filled blanks and vital figures and writing. Helps avoid unau-thorized additions or changes on portions of document where it is applied.

NOTE. A written agreement to pay a certain sum of money at a specified time.

NOTICE OF DISHONOR. A notice given in connection with a nego-tiable instrument that is in default. Consult local area banking authorities.

NOTICE OF NON-RESPONSIBILITY. A document, in form specified by law, signed by the owner of real estate, in which the owner declares that he will not be responsible to pay for work done on or supplies delivered to his property which have been ordered or contracted for by another such as a lessee.

NOTICE OF PROTEST. A notice given in connection with a negoti-able instrument that has been dishonored. Consult local area banking authorities.

O

OATH. A solemn pledge or promise, containing reference to a Su-preme Being. A person who intentionally makes false statements under oath is punishable for perjury.

OBLIGATION. 1. A legal or moral duty to do or not do something. 2. A sum of money the obligor has agreed to pay.

OBLIGEE. 1. A person or entity for whom something is done or not done. 2. A person or entity to whom money is owed in connection with an obligation.

OBLIGOR. 1. A person or entity who has agreed to do or not do something. 2. A person or entity who owes money in connection with an obligation.

OBSOLETE. Out of date. No longer used. Archaic.

OFFER. 1. To make a proposal. 2. A proposal.

OFFICIAL ACT. An act performed by a qualified person who is ap-pointed or elected to serve the public.

OFFICIAL CHARACTER, CERTIFICATE OF. See CERTIFICATE OF AUTHORITY.

OLOGRAPHIC. See HOLOGRAPHIC WILL.

OMISSION. A failure to perform a duty. See INSURANCE POLICY, NOTARY ERRORS AND OMISSIONS INSURANCE, NONFEA-SANCE.

OPTION. 1. An agreement to keep an offer open for a specified time. 2. A paid privilege allowing the person with the option the right to buy or sell something at a fixed price and time. 3. The power or right to make a choice.

ORDINARY CARE. See REASONABLE CARE.

ORIGINAL. Pertaining to documents, the first one made; one from which a copy or reproduction might be made.

P

PARISH. An area within a state whose boundaries are determined by political and population considerations. See COUNTY, BOROUGH.

PARTNER. A member of a partnership.

PARTNERSHIP AGREEMENT. An agreement made between two or more people. Consult local area legal counsel.

PARTY (PARTIES). 1. A person or group taking part in a legal agreement, transaction, or proceeding. 2. A litigant.

PARTY PROVEN. See ACKNOWLEDGMENT, CERTIFICATE OF, (PARTY PROVEN ON OATH OF SUBSCRIBING WITNESS).

PASSPORT. A document issued by a government, to be used as evidence or proof that the person in whose name it is issued is a citizen of the issuing country.

PATENT. 1. A document issued by the United States Patent and Trademark Office, granting to the inventor or his agent the exclusive right to manufacture, sell, and use an invention described in the Patent in the United States. 2. A document used by the government in connection with the conveyance of public land. Consult local area real estate authorities.

PAYABLE. Money to be paid.

PAYEE. The person who receives payment.

PAYMENT. 1. Satisfaction of a debt by any means accepted by the payee. 2. A specific sum of money.

PAYOR. The person who pays.

PENALTY. 1. Punishment. 2. A sum of money to be paid if a person or entity fails to fulfill the terms of an agreement.

PERJURY. 1. The crime, usually considered a felony, of falsely swearing or wilfully violating an oath or affirmation. See AFFIRMATION, OATH. 2. A false statement made under oath or affirmation.

PER SE. Latin. "By himself or in itself. Standing alone."

PERSON. A human being or other entity recognized by law as having the capacity to defend its rights or prosecute its claims.

PERSONAL PROPERTY. All property that is not real property. See REAL PROPERTY.

PERSONALLY KNOWN TO ME. See KNOWN TO ME TO BE.

PETITION. 1. A formal request made for the purpose of asking another for rights or privileges. 2. To make a formal request to correct, change, or remedy. 3. To make a claim for damages.

PHYSICAL DISABILITY. See COMPETENCE, INCOMPETENCE.

PLAINTIFF. The party who initiates a lawsuit. See DEFENDANT.

PLAT OF SURVEY. A map. Consult local area real estate authorities.

PLAT OF TOWNSHIP. A map. Consult local area real estate authorities.

PLEADINGS. Formal statements or declarations made by an advocate in support of a cause. Consult local area legal counsel.

POWER. The right, ability, or authority to do something.

POWER OF ATTORNEY. A document by which a person (called the principal) grants power or authorizes another (called the attorney-in-fact or agent) to act in his behalf. Also called Letter of Attorney. Consult local area legal counsel.

PRACTICE. 1. A repeated or customary action. 2. To perform repeatedly or customarily. 3. To engage in a business or profession. 4. A business or profession.

PRECEPTS OF GOOD NOTARY PRACTICE. Practices and ethical procedures recommended for Notaries Public by the National Notary Association.

PRESENTMENT. 1. The act of demanding payment in connection with a negotiable instrument. Consult local area banking authorities. 2. A report made by a jury.

PRIMA FACIE. Latin. "At first view." Presumed to be true. Consult local area legal counsel.

PRINCIPAL. 1. A legal entity whose performance is guaranteed by the surety company. Also called the obligor. See NOTARY BOND, SURETY BOND. 2. The one who gives authority to an agent. See POWER OF ATTORNEY. 3. The amount of a loan.

PRINCIPLE. A fundamental general statement accepted as basic and incontrovertible.

PROBATE. A court procedure in connection with the administration of affairs and distribution of the property of a deceased person. Consult local area legal counsel.

PROMISSORY NOTE. A written agreement that contains a promise to pay a specified sum of money on demand or at a specified time. Consult local area banking authorities.

PRONOTARY. See PROTHONOTARY.

PROOF, CERTIFICATE OF. See ACKNOWLEDGMENT, CERTIFICATE OF, (PARTY PROVEN ON OATH OF SUBSCRIBING WITNESS).

PROOF OF ACKNOWLEDGMENT. See ACKNOWLEDGMENT, CERTIFICATE OF, (PARTY PROVEN ON OATH OF SUBSCRIBING WITNESS).

PROPERTY. Anything owned. See PERSONAL PROPERTY, REAL PROPERTY.

PROSECUTE. 1. To do what is considered necessary to accomplish an objective. 2. To take action in a court proceeding.

PROTEST. See NOTICE OF PROTEST.

PROTHONOTARY. The title given to a public official whose duties include keeping records of Notaries and furnishing certificates of authority for notarized documents.

PROVE. To establish the truth by presenting evidence and/or testimony.

PROVEN PARTY. See ACKNOWLEDGMENT, CERTIFICATE OF (PARTY PROVEN ON OATH OF A SUBSCRIBING WITNESS).

PROXIMATE CAUSE. 1. An event or act, without which, the resulting accident and/or damages could not have occurred. 2. Any event or act which, if continued, in the normal course of events will cause a foreseeable occurrence or result. Consult local area legal counsel.

PUBLIC. 1. Citizens of the United States. 2. Anything that may be used, viewed, or inspected by a citizen of the United States. Not private. 3. All the people who have rights, privileges, duties and obligations within a community, state or nation.

PUBLIC DOCUMENT. Any document open to the public for inspection. See COUNTY RECORDER.

PUBLIC OFFICER. A person holding office in which he is presumed to serve the public.

PUBLIC RECORD. Any record open to the public for inspection. See COUNTY RECORDER.

PUNISH A WITNESS. A duty or power relating to witnesses who disobey subpoenas. Obsolete term. Consult local area legal counsel.

PUNITIVE DAMAGES. Exemplary damages.

PURSUANT. To carry out. Regarding. According to.

Q

QUALIFICATION. A requisite or characteristic that makes a person or thing suitable to serve or to be used for a specific purpose.

QUALIFIED. See QUALIFICATION.

QUASI. Latin. "As if, as it were." Used as a prefix; indicates some resemblance to, but not an identity with, the word to which it is prefixed.

QUITCLAIM DEED. A deed by which the right, title and interest in property is released or given up (rather than granted or warranted) to another. See DEED, GRANT DEED, WARRANTY DEED.

R

RATIFICATION. A formal act of adopting, approving or sanctioning.

RATIFY. To formally adopt, approve or sanction.

REAL ESTATE. Real property.

REAL PROPERTY. Property that includes land, buildings, and permanent installations on the land (such as fences). Also called real estate and realty.

REALTOR®. A service mark used by a person who is a member of the National Association of Real Estate Boards.

REALTY. Real property.

REASONABLE CARE. The degree of care expected of an ordinarily prudent person of average intelligence in a given situation. Also known as Ordinary Care.

RECOMMENDATION. A statement concerning another's worthiness, good character, and/or moral integrity.

RECONVEYANCE. The transfer of title to land back to the debtor after a mortgage or trust deed has been paid. Consult local area real estate and banking authorities.

RECORD BOOK, NOTARY. See JOURNAL OF NOTARIAL ACTS.

RECORDER OF PUBLIC DOCUMENTS. A public officer whose duties include the preservation, safekeeping, and preparation of certified copies of public documents. Also called a County Recorder and Custodian of Public Documents or Records.

REDEMPTION. Purchase of property that has been encumbered. Consult local area real estate and banking authorities.

REFERENDUM. The democratic process that allows the public to approve or reject a proposed measure or law by secret ballot.

REGISTER. A written record of any facts that may be considered important. See JOURNAL.

REGULATION. A rule or order, sometimes having the force of law.

REIMBURSE. To pay back the same or an equivalent amount.

RELEASE. 1. To surrender or give up a right or claim. 2. The surrendering or giving up of a right or claim.

REMOVAL. 1. Dismissal from office. 2. Change of location of office.

RENUNCIATION (RENOUNCIATION). A declaration of abandonment of rights to property. Consult local area legal counsel.

RESCIND. 1. To void or cancel an agreement by declaring that it never existed. 2. To void or cancel an agreement by restoring conditions existing before the agreement took effect. Consult local area legal counsel.

RESIDE. To live permanently in a fixed place.

RESIGNATION. The formal statement of one's intention to terminate an appointment and cease performing the duties of the office.

RESPONDENT. A person who is involved in a lawsuit. A litigant. Consult local area legal counsel.

RESPONSIBILITY. The obligation to be held accountable to indemnify those who suffer damages.

RESPONSIBLE. See RESPONSIBILITY.

REVOCATION. See REVOKE.

REVOKE. 1. To terminate a person's commission or appointment prior to its normal expiration. 2. To cancel or void.

RICHARD ROE. A person whose name is not known.

RIGHT. 1. Correct. 2. Something to which a person has a fair and just claim. 3. Qualities that are considered reasonable, acceptable, fair and just.

RIGHT TO DIE DECLARATION. A formal written statement in which the signer declares that he be allowed to die in the event that he becomes physically or mentally incompetent. Also known as a Living Will. Consult local area legal counsel.

RUBBER STAMP SEAL. 1. A rubber stamp that, when inked and pressed on paper makes the imprint of a seal. 2. The imprint made by the rubber stamp seal. See SEAL.

RULES OF NOTARIAL PRACTICE. Nationwide ethical and procedural guidelines, promulgated by the National Notary Association. See NOTARIAN™.

S

/S/. Used in conforming a copy to indicate that a person signed in the place where the name has been typed next to /S/. See CONFORM.

S.S. Abbreviation for scilicet.

SAFE DEPOSIT BOX. A box or safe in the vaults of a banking facility which can be rented to be used for safekeeping of valuables. Consult local area banking authorities.

SCILICET. Latin. "to wit, namely." Abbreviated "S.S." and printed near the venue of a certificate of acknowledgment. It is falling into disuse.

SCRAWL. See SCROLL.

SCROLL. A written design used in place of a written signature or seal. Also called a Scrawl.

SEAL. 1. An identifying mark, symbol, logo and/or lettering, embossed, printed or written on a document by an official (such as a Notary) as additional evidence that an official act (such as a notarization) has been performed. See EMBOSSER SEAL, EMBOSSMENT, RUBBER STAMP SEAL, SCROLL. 2. A plier-like device that makes an embossment of a seal on paper. See EMBOSSER SEAL. 3. A rubber stamp that makes an imprint of a seal on paper. See RUBBER STAMP SEAL.

SEARCH OF TITLE. See TITLE SEARCH.

SECURITY. 1. Property that is pledged to another to guarantee payment of a debt. Consult local area banking authorities. 2. A bond or stock.

SEQUENTIAL. Indicia, numbers or letters listed in a logical order.

SHORTHAND REPORTER. A person who uses some form of rapid writing in abbreviated form to record testimony and then transcribes it, so that it can be read.

SIC. Latin. "thus, so." Deliberately written thus. Reproduced exactly as originally written.

SIGHT DRAFT. A note payable when presented to the payor. A negotiable instrument. Consult local area banking authorities.

SIGILLUM. Latin. "seal." Seal. See LOCUS SIGILLI.

SIGN. To write one's name by hand.

SIGNATORY. A person who signs his name.

SIGNATURE. 1. A person's name in his own handwriting. 2. A mark (usually an "x") made in place of signature by a person who cannot sign his name. See SIGNATURE BY MARK.

SIGNATURE BY MARK. See SIGNATURE, ACKNOWLEDG- MENT, CERTIFICATE OF.

SIGNATURE GUARANTEED. A phrase stamped on a document (such as a stock transfer agreement) signed by a bank officer, stat- ing that the signature on the document is the true signature of the person making a request for funds or transfer. Consult local area banking authorities and securities and exchange commission. See ENDORSEMENT GUARANTEED.

SIGNUM. Latin. "Sign, mark, seal."

SPECIMEN. A sample or copy used to demonstrate what the original looks like.

STATEMENT. 1. A declaration. 2. An oral or written presentation or report.

STATUTE. A law.

STATUTE OF FRAUDS. See FRAUDS, STATUTE OF.

STATUTE OF LIMITATIONS. See LIMITATIONS, STATUTE OF.

SUBCONTRACT. A secondary and subordinate contract made be- tween one party to the original contract and a third party to per- form work or carry out obligations. Consult local area legal coun- sel.

SUBLEASE. A secondary and subordinate lease between the tenant of an original lease and a third party. Consult local area legal counsel.

SUBPOENA. Latin. "under penalty." A formal order issued by a court demanding attendance in court.

SUBROGATION. The act of allowing one who has paid a claim or obligation for another, to assume the othe 's rights and obligations so that he may try to recover part or al. ѹ the sums paid. Consult local area real estate and insurance authorities.

SUBSCRIBE. To sign. To write one's signature.

SUBSCRIBING WITNESS. A witness who signs. See ACKNOWL-EDGMENT, CERTIFICATE OF, (ON OATH OF SUBSCRIBING WITNESS), (PARTY PROVEN ON OATH OF SUBSCRIBING WITNESS).

SURETY BOND. An agreement (called a bond) signed by a surety company (called the obligor) and an entity (called the principal) in which the surety company agrees to indemnify an entity (called the obligee) if the principal fails to properly perform acts in connection with an agreement, office or undertaking. The surety company can demand reimbursement from the principal if it is required to indemnify the obligee. See NOTARY BOND.

SUMMONS. A formal order issued by a court demanding attendance in court.

SURNAME. Last name; family name.

SURROGATE. A judicial officer, usually with local jurisdiction, who administers matters of probate and guardianship. Also known as Judge of Probate, Register, Judge of the Orphan's Court.

SWEAR. To make a pledge solemnized by reference to a Supreme Being. See OATH.

T

TENANCY IN COMMON. The ownership of property by two or more persons in an agreement which, by law, transfers ownership to heirs or devisees rather than to the survivor(s) upon the death of one of the owners. Consult local area legal counsel. See COMMUNITY PROPERTY, JOINT TENANCY.

TENDER. 1. To offer. 2. The offer of money, property, or services.

TERM. The maximum time for which an elected or appointed office may be held without re-election or re-appointment.

TESTAMENT. See WILL.

TESTATOR. A person who makes or has made a will.

TESTIFY. To give testimony under oath or affirmation in a legal proceeding.

TESTIMONIUM CLAUSE. At the end of many documents, a clause

that follows the form: "In witness whereof, I have hereunto set my hand and seal this ___ day of ___ 19 ___," or "Witness my hand and seal."

TESTIMONY. 1. Evidence given under oath or affirmation in a legal proceeding. 2. A solemn oral declaration usually given in response to questions.

TITLE. 1. Proof or evidence of ownership of property. See TITLE SEARCH, TITLE INSURANCE POLICY. 2. A distinguishing name given to a person to signify that he holds some office or qualifications not possessed by others. 3. A number, descriptive heading or caption used to identify or classify a document.

TITLE, ABSTRACT OF. See TITLE SEARCH.

TITLE INSURANCE POLICY. An insurance policy issued by a title insurance company (insuror) who agrees to indemnify the insured (usually a buyer of real estate) in the event that information reported in a title search is incorrect or the documents containing that information are found to be fraudulent or counterfeit. Consult local area real estate authorities and title insurance companies.

TITLE SEARCH. A preliminary report made, (usually by a title insurance company) after an inspection of all records, to discover fraudulent or counterfeit documents and report encumbrances, rights and claims against property to a prospective buyer or owner. Also called Search of Title and Abstract of Title. Consult local area real estate authorities and title insurance companies.

TORT. A wrong doing.

TOWNSHIP. An area within a state whose boundaries are determined by political and population considerations.

TO WIT. That is to say; namely.

TRADEMARK. 1. A distinctive letter, word or mark used to identify and distinguish a particular service or product from any other offered. Also called a Service Mark. 2. The exclusive right to use a distinguishing letter, mark or design given to the user by the United States Patent and Trademark Office.

TRANSACTION. An act or agreement made between two or more entities.

TRANSCRIBE. 1. To put in writing. 2. To make a copy that is readable of something dictated or recorded in shorthand.

TRANSCRIPT. The writing resulting from the act of transcribing. See TRANSCRIBE.

TRANSFER. 1. To change possession or control to another, especially of title to property. 2. A conveyance.

TRANSLATE. To make a translation. See INTERPRETER.

TRANSLATION. A document that contains a writing in one language and its interpretation in another language. See INTERPRETATION.

TRANSLATION, CERTIFIED. See CERTIFIED TRANSLATION.

TRUST. A right, title or interest in property granted by the trustor to the trustee for the benefit of another called the beneficiary.

TRUSTEE. The one who retains control of property for another. See TRUST, TRUST DEED.

TRUSTOR. The one who grants rights, title or interest in property to another. See TRUST, TRUST DEED.

TRUST DEED. A legal form that permits a borrower (the trustor) to retain control of property by transferring the title to another (the trustee) during the time the loan is outstanding. In the event the borrower defaults, the trustee is required to transfer title and possession of the property to the lender (the beneficiary). Consult local area real estate and banking authorities.

TURPITUDE, MORAL. See MORAL TURPITUDE.

U

UNBIASED. Impartial. Unprejudiced. See IMPARTIAL WITNESS.

UNFAIR. Not fair and just.

UNDUE INFLUENCE. Wrongful exertion of will and persuasion over another to cause him to do, stop doing or not do something. Consult local area legal counsel.

UNIFORM NOTARY ACT. Practices and procedures in the form of a model state Notary act drafted by a national committee composed of legislators, attorneys, and representatives of Yale Legislative Services and the National Notary Association.

UNIFORM RECOGNITION OF ACKNOWLEDGMENTS ACT. Draft legislation approved and recommended for enactment by the National Conference of Commissioners on Uniform State Laws, relating to those officers qualified to take acknowledgments of United States citizens resident in one state, who are temporarily residing in another state or foreign country.

UNIFORM STATE LAWS. Proposals for legislation that could be enacted by a state legislature, drafted by the National Conference of Commissioners on Uniform State Laws, a group composed of attorneys-at-law. See UNIFORM RECOGNITION OF ACKNOWLEDGMENTS ACT.

UNJUST. That which is unfair. Wrongful. See FAIR AND JUST.

UNLAWFUL. Not permitted by law.

UNWRITTEN LAW. See COMMON LAW.

V

VACATE. 1. To resign from an office or appointment. 2. To move one's office out of the area (jurisdiction) within which one is allowed or permitted to perform the duties connected with an appointment or office.

VALID. Legally binding. In effect.

VALIDITY. See VALID.

VENDEE. Buyer.

VENDOR. Seller.

VENUE. 1. The place where an act is performed. 2. The place on a Notary certificate that gives the location where the notarial act was performed. 3. The place where a trial is held.

VERIFICATION. 1. A certified copy. 2. A certificate of acknowledgment. 3. An oath or affirmation administered by an official to an affiant. 4. The statements or declarations made by a person, who may have taken an oath or affirmation, concerning the truth of another's testimony or the genuineness of evidence. 5. A notarization. 6. An affidavit of authenticity. A term whose definition varies widely as used in the United States.

VERIFY. See VERIFICATION.

VESTED INTEREST. 1. An additional right or interest that, if acquired, would result in absolute and unconditional ownership. 2. A strong personal commitment.

VIOLATE. 1. To break the law. 2. To fail to perform as agreed.

VISA. A permit that allows the bearer to enter a foreign country.

VOID. Having no force or effect.

VOIDABLE. Capable of being made void.

VOLUNTARY ACT. An act done intentionally and willingly. Not coerced or unduly influenced. Of one's own choice. See ACKNOWLEDGMENT.

VOTE. To formally and voluntarily express approval or disapproval of a proposal, option, or candidate for office.

VOTER. 1. A person with the right or qualifications to vote. 2. A person who exercises his right to vote.

W

WAIVE. To relinquish or give up voluntarily.

WARRANTY. A guarantee given by a grantor to the grantee stating that the grantor will be responsible to the grantee if certain facts are not true or certain events do not occur.

WARRANTY DEED. A deed given with a warranty. See QUITCLAIM DEED, GRANT DEED. Consult local area legal counsel.

WILFUL. Intentional; deliberate.

WILL. A document signed by the maker (testator) that gives directions regarding the administration, control and disposal of the testator's property on his death. Also called a Last Will and Testament. Consult local area legal counsel.

WITNESS. 1. A person who observes an event. 2. A person who gives testimony under oath. See ATTEST.

WRIT. A formal document issued by authority of a court. Consult local area legal counsel.

WRONG. A harmful, incorrect, unfair and unjust act. A tort. A wrongdoing. Wrongful.

WRONGDOING. See WRONG.

WRONGFUL. See WRONG.

X, Y, Z

X. See SIGNATURE BY MARK.

Benjamin Harrison

President of the United States of America

To all who shall see these Presents, Greeting:

Know Ye, That, reposing special trust and confiden[ce]

I do appoint him to be _Notary_ _Public_ _for_ _the_ _District_ of

fulfill the duties of that Office according to Law, and

privileges, and emoluments thereunto of right appertaining u[nto]

term of five years from the date hereof.

In testimony whereof, I have caused these Letters to

to be hereunto affixed.

Given under my hand, at the City of Washington, the —21st— [day]

Lord one thousand eight hundred and ninety three,

of America the 117th.

By the President:

Attorney General.

in the *Integrity* and *Ability* of *Milton C. Barnard*

Columbia; and do authorize and empower him to execute and

have and to hold the said *Office,* with all the powers,

him, the said *Milton C. Barnard* for the

made *Patent* and the seal of the *Department* of *Justice*

of *February* , in the year of our

and of the *Independence* of the *United States*

Benj Harrison

Benjamin Harrison's signature on this turn-of-the-century notarial commission certificate of 1893 testifies to the significance of the notarial office. In the District of Columbia, the President of the United States granted notarial commissions until the Commissioner of the District took over that responsibility.

APPENDICES

INTRODUCTION TO APPENDICES

In most other countries the Notary Public law is promulgated and administered by the central governing agency for all citizens of the country. In the United States, the Notary Public law and its administration are delegated to an appointed or elected officer in each state. In 1973, the National Notary Association organized a committee of lawyers and legislators, and together with Yale Legislative Services of Yale Law School, drafted a Uniform Notary Act to be used as a model in any state considering the modernization of its existing Notary law. Several of the states have already enacted substantial sections of the Uniform Notary Act. Appendix A contains the 1976 first revision of *Draft Legislation for a Uniform Notary Act.*

In January 1977 the National Notary Association filed the word NOTARIAN™ in the United States Office of Trademarks and Patents. The title of NOTARIAN™ is permitted to be used by those Notaries Public who take and pass a written examination and further obligate themselves to perform notarial acts competently and above and beyond the requirements specified in the law. As a NOTARIAN™, the Notary Public is cognizant of his unique role of public officer and impartial witness. He must disqualify himself from acting in connection with any transaction for which he might later be accused of serving in the inconsistent dual roles of agent or advocate and impartial witness. Appendix B contains the RULES OF NOTARIAL PRACTICE.

Because of the relative ease of qualifying and becoming a Notary Public, people from the professions of law, accountancy, banking, insurance, real estate and finance often perform notarial acts for the convenience of their *customers* and *clients*. Two words are italicized in the last sentence as a reminder that the Notary Public is appointed as a ministerial officer of the state and in this role is obligated to serve his "constituents" as an impartial witness. Appendix C contains a list of national organizations and associations whose members often qualify as Notaries Public.

Appendix D lists the names and addresses of the officer who appoints Notaries Public in each state and the District of Columbia.

Appendix E lists the approximate number of commissioned Notaries Public in each of the 50 states and the District of Columbia.

Appendix F contains the suggested form for several of the less commonly used certificates of acknowledgment, Certified Copy and instructions for filling out a certificate of acknowledgment.

Appendix A

Draft Legislation and Commentary for a Uniform Notary Act

UNIFORM NOTARY ACT ADVISORY COMMITTEE*

ALLEN J. BEERMANN, Secretary of State, Nebraska

DANIEL E. BOATWRIGHT, Assemblyman, California

EUGENE A. BURDICK, Judge, State District Court, North Dakota

HAROLD J. HERTZBERG, Attorney at Law, California

NORMAN JENSEN, Attorney at Law, California

JOHN A. JUDGE, Attorney at Law, California

JOSEPH C. MASCARI, Attorney at Law, California

JACK MURATORI, Deputy Secretary of State, New York

ALAN ROBBINS, State Senator, California

EDWARD RUBIN, Attorney at Law, California

CHARLES J. WEISSBURD, Chief Deputy Registrar-Recorder, California

FRED L. WINELAND, Secretary of State, Maryland

NATIONAL NOTARY ASSOCIATION: Raymond C. Rothman and Milton G. Valera

YALE LEGISLATIVE SERVICES, YALE LAW SCHOOL: John Adney, Arthur J. Silverstein and Mark D. Turkel

---

*Public spirited individuals and organizations who contributed their time and expertise generously and without monetary gain.

The Uniform Notary Act Advisory Committee, as a group, does not endorse, recommend, or lobby for, or against adoption of any part or all of the Draft Legislation For A Uniform Notary Act.

The opinions expressed in the Commentary to the Draft Legislation For A Uniform Notary Act do not necessarily represent those of the Advisory Committee or any individual, organization, office or agency.

PREFACE
A Uniform Notary Law

Because the United States is today a highly integrated and interdependent society, commercial and cultural distinctions which once existed between the states have, to a large extent, disappeared. Thus, there is a great need to modernize and make uniform the various state notary public statutes because:

1. Acts of notaries public are likely to have interstate implications, and,

2. Original justifications for diverse notary public laws have become anachronisms in today's society.

A Uniform Notary Law, drafted to meet the commercial and societal needs of the Twentieth Century, would bring all state notary public statutes into conformity.

All fifty States and the District of Columbia have enacted statutes concerning notaries public. Many of these laws were passed during the late Eighteenth and Nineteenth Centuries and, to a large extent (despite subsequent modifications), still reflect the commercial and cultural needs of that era. Additionally, many notary statutes also reflect distinctions among the states. For example, Louisiana, with its predominantly French origins, accords much greater status and powers to notaries public than those states such as Connecticut which followed the English common law. Various state notary statutes differ widely in scope; some states have comprehensive legislation regulating notaries public, others have laws which establish only minimal guidelines concerning notaries public. The latter, for example, often omit significant provisions with respect to procedural duties of notaries public in performing their official acts, as well as rules governing the liabilities of notaries public and their removal from office.

This proposed Uniform Notary Act is designed to meet the commercial and societal needs of the Twentieth Century by bringing all state notary public statutes into conformity, and, through its detailed provisions, to clarify and define the role of the notary public in modern society.

The Uniform Notary Act has been drafted as a comprehensive piece of legislation designed to encompass all facets of the law concerning notaries public. The Act is divided into eight Articles dealing with (I) General Provisions, (II) Appointment Provisions, (III) Powers, (IV) Duties, (V) Forms and Procedures, (VI) Liability, Fines and Imprisonment, (VII) Revocation of Commission, Action for Injunction, Unauthorized Practice of Law, and (VIII) Certificate of Authority. These Articles are further subdivided into parts and sections for quick reference.

The language of the statute is uncomplicated and easily comprehended by laymen who, to a great extent, constitute the ranks of notaries public in this country.

First Draft September, 1973
Second Draft August, 1974
First Revision January, 1976

Uniform Notary Act

Title

An Act

To be known as the Uniform Notary Act, relating to the appointment, qualifications, powers, duties, liabilities and removal of notaries public; to make uniform the Law with respect thereto; and to repeal inconsistent legislation.

Article, Part and Section Analysis

ARTICLE I — General Provisions
Part I   Short Title, Purposes and Rules of Construction, Prospective Effect of Act, Construction Against Implicit Repeal, Notary Public and Notarization Defined, Severability, Repeal, Time of Taking Effect

SECTION —
1-101   Short Title
1-102   Purposes and Rules of Construction
1-103   Prospective Effect of Act
1-104   Construction Against Implicit Repeal
1-105   Notary Public and Notarization Defined
1-106   Severability
1-107   Repeal
1-108   Time of Taking Effect

ARTICLE II — Appointment Provisions
Part I   Appointment, Jurisdiction and Term, Local or District Offices

SECTION —
2-101   Appointment
2-102   Jurisdiction and Term

2-103   Local or District Offices

Part II   Application, Qualifying Fee, Applicant's Endorsers, Applicant's Affirmation, Bond, Confidential
Application, Specimen Official Signature
SECTION —
2-201   Application
2-202   Qualifying Fee
2-203   Applicant's Endorsers
2-204   Applicant's Affirmation
2-205   Bond
2-206   Confidential Application
2-207   Specimen Official Signature

Part III   State and Local Government Employees
SECTION —
2-301   State and Local Government Employees

ARTICLE III — Powers

Part I   Powers, Limitations on Powers
SECTION —
3-101   Powers
3-102   Limitations on Powers

ARTICLE IV — Duties

Part I   Journal, Entries in Journal, Signature in Journal,
Facsimiles of Records; Duty to Furnish
SECTION —
4-101   Journal
4-102   Entries in Journal
4-103   Signature in Journal
4-104   Facsimiles of Records; Duty to Furnish

Part II   Official Signature, Rubber Stamp Seal, Seal Embosser, Illegibility
SECTION —

1   4-201   Official Signature
2   4-202   Rubber Stamp Seal
3   4-203   Seal Embosser
4   4-204   Illegibility
5   Part III   Change of Address, Change of Notary's Name,
6   Lost Journal or Official Seal
7   SECTION —
8   4-301   Change of Address
9   4-302   Change of Notary's Name
10   4-303   Lost Journal or Official Seal
11   Part IV   Notice and Maximum Fees
12   SECTION —
13   4-401   Notice and Maximum Fees
14   Part V   Death, Resignation or Removal, Revocation of
15   Commission, Failure to be Reappointed, Reap-
16   pointment
17   SECTION —
18   4-501   Death
19   4-502   Resignation or Removal
20   4-503   Revocation of Commission
21   4-504   Failure to be Reappointed
22   4-505   Reappointment
23
24   ARTICLE V —   Forms and Procedures
25   Part I   Acknowledgment Forms; Affirmation: Procedure,
26   Form; Executing Witness Form; Certified Fac-
27   similes of Documents: Procedure, Form
28   SECTION —
29   5-101   Acknowledgment Forms
30   5-102   Affirmation: Procedure, Form
31   5-103   Executing Witness Form
32   5-104   Certified Facsimiles of Documents: Pro-
33   cedure, Form

1   *ARTICLE VI* – Liability, Fines and Imprisonment
2   Part I   Liability of Notary and Sureties, Liability of
3   Employer of Notary, Proximate Cause
4   SECTION –
5   6-101   Liability of Notary and Sureties
6   6-102   Liability of Employer of Notary
7   6-103   Proximate Cause
8   Part II   Official Misconduct Defined, Official Misconduct,
9   Willful Impersonation, Wrongful Possession
10   SECTION –
11   6-201   Official Misconduct Defined
12   6-202   Official Misconduct
13   6-203   Willful Impersonation
14   6-204   Wrongful Possession
15
16   *ARTICLE VII* –Revocation of Commission, Action for Injunc-
17   tion, Unauthorized Practice of Law
18   Part I   Revocation of Commission
19   SECTION –
20   7-101   Revocation of Commission
21   Part II   Action for Injunction, Unauthorized Practice of
22   Law, Remedies Additional to Those Now Existing
23   SECTION –
24   7-201   Action for Injunction, Unauthorized
25   Practice of Law
26   7-202   Remedies Additional to Those Now Ex-
27   isting
28
29   *ARTICLE VIII* –Certificate of Authority
30   Part I   Certificate of Authority
31   SECTION –
32   8-101   Certificate of Authority
33

Commentary — Article I

This article contains such general provisions as a short title for the Act; certain guidelines for judicial construction, including an instruction reasonably to avoid the implicit alteration or repeal of any segment of the Act; and a standard severability clause. Article I specifies that the Act has prospective effect only, but this includes renewals of existing commissions (though the Act does not in itself evoke any existing commission). The term "notary public" is defined to indicate that only an individual—not a corporation, partnership or other legal entity—can become a notary public.

The District of Columbia, the Commonwealth of Puerto Rico and any territory or possession of the United States may be substituted for the word "state" throughout the Act where applicable.

Article I
Part I

§ 1-101   Short Title

This Act shall be known and may be cited as the Uniform Notary Act.

§ 1-102   Purposes and Rules of Construction

(a) This Act shall be construed and applied to promote its underlying purposes and policies.

(b) The underlying purposes and policies of this Act are:

(1) to simplify, clarify, and modernize the law governing notaries public;

(2) to make uniform notary laws among the states enacting it;

(3) to promote, serve, and protect the public interest.

(c) In this Act, unless the context otherwise requires,

1   (1) words in the singular number include the plural, and

2   words in the plural number include the singular;

3   (2) words of the masculine gender include the feminine

4   and the neuter;

5   (3) words of the neuter gender may refer to any gender

6   when the sense so indicates.

7   § 1-103   Prospective Effect of Act

8   This Act applies prospectively. Nothing in this Act shall be

9   construed to revoke any notary public commission existing on the

10   effective date of this Act. All renewals of notarial commissions

11   shall be obtained in accordance with this Act.

12   § 1-104   Construction Against Implicit Repeal

13   This Act is intended to provide comprehensive and unified

14   coverage of the subject matter. Therefore, no part of it shall be

15   construed to be impliedly repealed or amended by subsequent

16   legislation if that construction can be avoided.

17   § 1-105   Notary Public and Notarization Defined

18   (a) The terms "notary public" or "notary" are used inter-

19   changeably to mean any individual appointed and com-

20   missioned to perform notarial acts.

21   (b) "Notarization" means the performance of a notarial act.

22   § 1-106   Severability

23   If any provision of this Act or the application thereof to any

24   person or circumstance is held invalid, the invalidity does not

25   affect other provisions or applications of the Act which can be

26   given effect without the invalid provision or application, and to

27   this end the provisions of this Act are severable.

28   § 1-107   Repeal

29   The following laws and parts of laws are hereby repealed:

30   (1) _____

31   (2) _____

32   § 1-108   Time of Taking Effect

33   This Act shall take effect _____

1   **Commentary — Article II**
2

3   *The words "appointing state official" appear throughout the*
4   *Act. This official is a state officer because the notary is*
5   *commissioned to act anywhere in the state. The appointing official*
6   *is commonly the Secretary of State.*
7   *The appointing official has no discretion to grant or deny an*
8   *application for appointment—the applicant is automatically com-*
9   *missioned, provided only that the application (including payment*
10   *of fees, submission of bond, taking of affirmation, etc.) is*
11   *complete and true. The appointing official may not, under*
12   *§ 2-101(b), commission an applicant who has not, by omission or*
13   *false representation, complied with all the requirements stated in*
14   *Part II of this Article. Further, a notary who is commissioned*
15   *despite his failure to comply with the requirements in Part II risks*
16   *having his commission revoked under § 7-101(1), which in turn*
17   *disqualifies him from making application for appointment until 10*
18   *years have lapsed from the date of the revocation, according to*
19   *§ 2-201(6). The 10 year rule in the last mentioned provision*
20   *applies, of course, to a revocation for any reason listed in § 7-101.*
21   *The powers and duties of a notary public as later enumerated*
22   *are basic and elementary. However, a notary public must employ*
23   *good judgment in the performance of all his notarial acts. Because*
24   *judgment and competence are qualities that are difficult if not*
25   *impossible to determine through general tests, this Act, through*
26   *deliberate omission, advocates the elimination of notary public*
27   *examinations.*
28   *Section 2-103 states that the appointing state official can*
29   *designate other offices in the state that he might need for*
30   *appointment of notaries public, record keeping purposes or to*
31   *issue Certificates of Authority.*
32   *Section 2-201 states that the applicant need only be registered*
33   *to vote in a state election in any of the United States, making it*

1   *possible for a person who is a registered voter in New York to*
2   *become a notary public in California, providing that he obtains the*
3   *signatures of three endorsers who are actually registered to vote in*
4   *California and provided that the applicant maintains a business or*
5   *residence office in California.*
6   *The applicant takes an affirmation that he has read and*
7   *understood the notary law. This affirmation is taken, and an*
8   *executed bond is submitted, in advance of the applicant's*
9   *appointment and commission by the appointing official. The*
10 *intention is to avoid unnecessary red tape for the notary applicant*
11 *and the appointing official, by having the applicant fulfill all*
12 *requirements at one time—the time of application—and before the*
13 *appointing official acts. As noted above, in most instances*
14 *commission will be issued as a matter of course, so that seldom*
15 *will the bond be submitted or the affirmation taken needlessly.*
16   *The Applicant's Affirmation Section 2-204 was changed by*
17 *amendment of January, 1976 to insure that the applicant cannot*
18 *easily obtain an additional notarial commission under an assumed*
19 *name.*
20   *Section 2-301 provides that the appointing state official may*
21 *waive the fee for appointment if the notary is to perform acts for*
22 *and in behalf of a government office only. However, a notary*
23 *commissioned under this section is subject to the remaining*
24 *provisions of the Act, e.g., he must file an application and keep a*
25 *journal, and he may incur liability under Article VI.*
26
27   Article II
28   Part I
29
30 § 2-101   Appointment
31   (a) Upon application under this Act, the [appointing state
32   official] may appoint and commission individual persons
33   as notaries public in this State.

1   (b) The [appointing state official] may not appoint and
2   commission as a notary public any person who submits an
3   application containing substantial and material misstate-
4   ment or omission of fact.
5   § 2-102   Jurisdiction and Term
6   Notaries public may perform notarial acts in any part of this State
7   for a term of four years, unless sooner removed.
8   § 2-103   Local or District Offices
9   The [appointing state official] may designate such local or district
10   offices within this State as he deems necessary for the public
11   convenience to provide certificates of authority and keep records
12   and specimen official signatures of notaries public whose business
13   or residence offices are located near the designated local or district
14   offices.
15   Part II
16
17   § 2-201   Application
18   Every applicant for appointment and commission as a notary
19   public shall complete an application to be filed with the
20   [appointing state official] stating:
21   (1) that he is a citizen of the United States, or if he is not a
22   citizen of the United States, that he is a citizen or national
23   of a country that permits American citizens to become
24   notaries public therein;
25   (2) if he is a citizen of the United States, that he is a qualified
26   elector of a State at the time of his application;
27   (3) that he is able to read and write English;
28   (4) the address of his business or residence in this State;
29   (5) his social security number, if he has one; and
30   (6) that during the past [10] years his commission as a notary
31   public has not been revoked.
32   § 2-202   Qualifying Fee
33   Every applicant for appointment and commission as a notary

1   public shall pay to the [appointing state official] a fee of [$6]

2   § 2-203   Applicant's Endorsers

3   Every applicant for appointment and commission as a notary

4   public shall submit to the [appointing state official] endorsements

5   from three qualified electors of this State, in the following form:

6   I,_____ [name of endorser], a qualified elector of this

7   State, believe, to the best of my knowledge, the applicant is a

8   person of good moral character and integrity and capable of

9   performing notarial acts.

10   _____

11   [Endorser's signature, address and social security number]

12   § 2-204   Applicant's Affirmation

13   *Every applicant for appointment and commission as a notary

14   public shall take the following affirmation in the presence of a

15   person qualified to administer an affirmation in this State:

16   I, _____ [name of applicant], solemnly affirm, under

17   the penalty of perjury, that the answers to all questions in this

18   application are true, complete and correct; that I have carefully

19   read the notary law of this State; and, if appointed and commis-

20   sioned as a notary public, I will perform faithfully, to the best of

21   my ability, all notarial acts in accordance with the law.

22   _____ [Signature of applicant]

23   Subscribed and affirmed before me this _____ day of _____ ,

24   19____ . The undersigned notary public further certifies that

25   _____ [name of applicant], is known to me to

26   be the applicant and elector who executed the within Application

27   for Appointment and Commission as a Notary Public and ac-

28   knowledged to me that [s]he executed the same for the purposes

29   therein stated.

30   _____ [Official signature and official seal of notary]

31   § 2-205   Bond

32   Every applicant for appointment and commission as a notary

33   public shall submit to the [appointing state official] an executed

*Revision January 1976

1   bond commencing at least 30 days after the date the applicant
2   mails his application to the [appointing state official] with a term
3   of [4] years, in the sum of [$5,000], with, as surety thereon, a
4   company qualified to write surety bonds in this State. The bond
5   shall be conditioned upon the faithful performance of all notarial
6   acts in accordance with this Act.
7   § 2-206   Confidential Application
8   Information in the application for appointment, except for the
9   applicant's name and address, is confidential and may not be
10   disclosed by an official or employee having access to it to any
11   person other than the applicant, his authorized representative, or
12   an employee or officer of the Federal Government, the State
13   Government, or a local agency, acting in his official capacity. Such
14   information shall be used by the [appointing state official] for the
15   sole purpose of performing his duties under this Act.
16   § 2-207   Specimen Official Signature
17   Every applicant for appointment and commission as a notary
18   public shall mail or deliver to the [appointing state official] a
19   handwritten specimen of his official signature which contains his
20   surname and at least the initial of his first name. The fee payable
21   to the [appointing state official] for recording a specimen of the
22   official signature is [$2]
23
24   **Part III**
25
26   § 2-301   State and Local Government Employees
27   (a) The [appointing state official] may appoint and commis-
28   sion such number of state and local government employees
29   as notaries public, to act for and in behalf of their
30   respective state and local government offices, as he deems
31   proper. An appointee commissioned as a notary public
32   under this section may act only for and in behalf of the
33   government office or offices in which he is employed.

1   (b) An appointee under this section shall meet the require-
2   ments for qualification and appointment prescribed in
3   Article II, Part II, except that the head of the state or local
4   government office where the applicant is employed may
5   execute a certificate that the application is made for the
6   purposes of the office and in the public interest and
7   submit it to the [appointing state official] together with
8   the application for appointment as a notary public, in
9   which case the fee for appointment specified in Section
10   2-202 is waived.
11   (c) Premium on the bond and costs of all other notary
12   supplies for a commissioned state or local government
13   employee shall be paid from funds available to the office
14   in which he is employed.
15   (d) All fees received for notarial services by a notary public
16   appointed for and in behalf of a state or local government
17   office shall be remitted by him to the state or local
18   government office in which he is employed.
19   (e) A notary public who is an employee of a state or local
20   government office in this State must comply with all
21   provisions of this Act.
22
23
24
25
26
27
28
29
30
31
32
33

Commentary — Article III

By completing a notary's certificate, the notary public makes it possible for the public-at-large to rely upon the authenticity of the person's signature (not the notary's signature) on the document, and be informed that the contents of the notarized document are intended to have force and effect.

When considering the effect of Section 3-102, it is necessary to keep in mind that the primary functions of the notary public are to identify the signer and witness his signature on the document. If there is a question of a disqualifying interest, it would be advisable to obtain the services of a disinterested notary public. Evaluate the following situations:

1. *The attorney-client relationship where the attorney, a notary public, is receiving a fee or retainer for drafting the document in addition to his fee, if any, as a notary public.*

2. *The officer of a corporation, stockholder of a corporation or bank officer who is a notary public, acting on behalf of his employer (the corporation or bank) who may be a party to the transaction directly or indirectly.*

3. *The real estate salesman-notary public who notarizes a deed in connection with the consummation of a sale of property where he will receive a commission in addition to his notarial fee.*

4. *The spouse-notary public who notarizes a document for his or her mate when the spouse-notary public could benefit directly, indirectly or not at all.*

After having considered carefully the responsibilities of a notary public and the possible disqualifying interest that arises in an attorney-notary public and client relationship, it would seem that the average attorney will turn to his secretary (rather than himself) to be appointed as a notary public.

1   **Article III**
2   **Part I**
3

4   § 3-101   Powers
5   (a) Every notary public is empowered to:
6   (1) take acknowledgments;
7   (2) administer oaths and affirmations;
8   (3) certify that a copy of a document is a true copy of
9   another document; and
10   (4) perform any other act permitted by law.
11   § 3-102   Limitations on Powers
12   (a) A notary public who has a disqualifying interest, as
13   hereinafter defined, in a transaction may not legally
14   perform any notarial act in connection with the trans-
15   action.
16   (b) For the purposes of this Act, a notary public has a
17   disqualifying interest in a transaction in connection with
18   which notarial services are requested if he:
19   (1) may receive directly, and as a proximate result of the
20   notarization, any advantage, right, title, interest, cash,
21   or property, exceeding in value the sum of any fee
22   properly received in accordance with Section 4-401 of
23   this Act, or
24   (2) is named, individually, as a party to the transaction.
25
26
27
28
29
30
31
32
33

Commentary — Article IV

This article contains a list of duties that the notary public is obliged to perform for the protection of the party who signed and for the public-at-large.

By keeping a journal of his notarial acts, the notary public makes it possible for anyone who questions the authenticity of the signature on the document at a later date to obtain evidence of such authenticity from the notary's journal that could be used in a legal action. The journal serves (1) to discourage forgers and impostors by requiring a signature in the journal that can be compared with the signatures on the document and on any identification cards presented; (2) to provide the notary with evidence (the person's signature in the journal) if it is later necessary for the notary to prove in court that the person actually appeared before him; and (3) to ensure that the person was properly identified by requiring the notary to enter evidence of identification in the journal. The pages of the journal must be numbered and irremovable so that entries cannot be made or pages inserted after the person whose signature has been notarized has left the notary's office.

Evidence of identity required in Section 4-102(5) is necessary to avoid forgery and impersonation. Sufficient evidence of identification should be requested and the information recorded in the notary's journal. Nothing has been included in this Act defining exactly what constitutes positive identification of an individual; this must ultimately be decided by a court of law. The notary public is obliged to perform his duties in such a way that this question will rarely need to be settled in a court of law. A person could present to the notary public, as evidence of his identity, one or more kinds of identification such as cards or passports. The notary is obligated to exercise the judgment of a prudent person of average intelligence to decide whether he should

1   *accept this evidence as satisfactory and sufficient. If the person is*
2   *personally known to the notary public as a friend, relative or*
3   *associate, no identification cards would be necessary. The friend's*
4   *appearance, voice, mannerisms and other physical characteristics*
5   *could provide the notary public with sufficient and satisfactory*
6   *evidence of identity.*
7   *The person's signature in the notary's journal is, of course,*
8   *always mandatory regardless of what methods or means are*
9   *accepted as satisfactory and sufficient for identification purposes.*
10   *By requiring in Section 4-103 that the person whose signature is*
11   *being notarized sign in the notary's journal, the forger and/or*
12   *impostor must duplicate his forgery at the time of the notarial act*
13   *on the document to be notarized and in the notary's journal. At*
14   *the time of the performance of the notarial act, the notary public*
15   *must carefully compare the person's signature on the identifica-*
16   *tion card or cards with those subscribed in the notary's presence*
17   *on the document and in the notary's journal.*
18   *The person whose signature is being notarized must appear*
19   *before the notary at the time of the notarization to subscribe his*
20   *name in the notary's journal to avoid the notary's fraudulent*
21   *certificate occasioned when a party presenting a document for*
22   *notarization attempts to circumvent the executing witness provi-*
23   *sions (§ 5-103), e.g., by assuring the notary: "My spouse signed*
24   *this deed at home, you can take my word for it."*
25   *Good business practice dictates that the notary public and the*
26   *persons whose signatures were notarized initial all corrections and*
27   *each page of the agreement in a corner as well as affix their*
28   *signatures in the proper place on the document and notary's*
29   *certificate.*
30   *Section 4-104 requires that a notary furnish facsimiles of his*
31   *journal or other records upon receipt of a written court order, and*
32   *only upon such order.*
33   *Section 4-202 introduces one of the most important innova-*

tions in notary law offered in this Act: it provides for the mandatory use of a rubber stamp seal capable of photographic reproduction. This change both updates notary law to take account of modern copying technology, and mandates uniform nationwide use of a manifestation of notarization (rubber stamp seal) that all persons may henceforth recognize.

The introduction of the rubber stamp seal overrules the long-standing use of the seal embosser, which §4-203 now makes optional. In earlier times, a "seal" was used in lieu of the personal signature, for many people did not know how to write their names. Today the seal embosser has an entirely different purpose and should be used in addition to the rubber stamp seal. The seal embosser makes indentations into paper that cannot be photo-graphically reproduced, thus helping to positively identify the document that was intended to be notarized from an altered machine copy that does not have the indentations made by the notary's seal embosser. If a document contains more than one page, the seal embosser should be used in a corner of each page. If there is not enough space on the document for the notary's certificate, the notary's loose certificate should be stapled to the document and the seal embosser should be used to squeeze the document and the notary's certificate together.

It should also be noted that reproduction of the Great Seal of the State is not prescribed on the rubber stamp seal or seal embosser.

Although illegibility of required information will not in itself invalidate a notarization (§4-204), an omission could affect its validity.

Article IV
Part I

§4-101.   Journal

Every notary public shall provide and keep a permanently-bound journal of his notarial acts containing numbered pages.

§ 4-102   Entries in Journal

Every notary public shall make a chronological list of all notarial acts in his journal. The information to be entered in the journal at the time of notarization shall include:

(1) the date and time of the notarial act;

(2) the type of notarial act performed;

(3) a description of the document, agreement, or proceeding;

(4) the printed name and address of each person whose signature is notarized;

(5) evidence of identity (including serial number of card and title of issuing authority, if available) exhibited to the notary public by the person whose signature is notarized; and

(6) other entries necessary by virtue of additional powers granted in Section 3-101.

§ 4-103   Signature in Journal

At the time of notarization, each person for whom a notarial act is to be performed shall sign his name in the notary's journal.

§ 4-104   Facsimiles of Records; Duty to Furnish

(a) "Facsimile" means an exact copy preserving all the written or printed marks of the original.

(b) Every notary public, upon written court order, shall furnish facsimiles of entries made in his journal of notarial acts or any other papers or copies relating to his notarial acts, upon receipt of a fee of _____ [suggested minimum $1 per 8½" x 11" page or part of a page].

Part II

§ 4-201   Official Signature

At the time of notarization a notary public shall sign his official

1 signature on every notary certificate.

2 § 4-202   Rubber Stamp Seal

3 Under or near his official signature on every notary certificate, a
4 notary public shall rubber stamp clearly and legibly, so that it is
5 capable of photographic reproduction:

6   (1) the words "Official Seal";
7   (2) his name exactly as he writes his official signature;
8   (3) the words "Notary Public", "State of [name of state]",
9   and "My commission expires [commission expiration
10   date]";
11   (4) the address of his business or residence in this State; and
12   (5) a serrated or milled edge border in a rectangular form not
13   more than [one inch in width by two and one-half inches
14   in length] surrounding the information.

15 § 4-203   Seal Embosser

16   (a) Every notary public may provide, keep, and use a seal
17   embosser engraved to show the words "Notary Seal", his
18   name, "Notary Public", and "State of [name of state]".

19   (b) The indentations made by the seal embosser shall not be
20   applied on the notarial certificate or document to be
21   notarized in a manner that will render illegible or incapable
22   of photographic reproduction any of the printed marks or
23   writing.

24 § 4-204   Illegibility

25 The illegibility of any of the information required by Sections
26 4-201 through 4-203 does not affect the validity of a transaction.

27

28   **Part III**

29

30 § 4-301   Change of Address

31 Every notary public shall mail or deliver notice to the [appointing
32 state official] within 30 days after he changes the address of his
33 business or residence in this State. The fee payable to the

1 [appointing state official] for recording notice of change of
2 address is [$2].
3 §4-302   Change of Notary's Name
4 Every notary public shall mail or deliver notice to the [appointing
5 state official] within 30 days after he changes his name, including
6 with the notification a specimen of his handwritten official
7 signature which contains his surname and at least the initial of his
8 first name. The fee payable to the [appointing state official] for
9 recording notice of change of notary's name is [$2].
10 §4-303   Lost Journal or Official Seal
11 Every notary public shall mail or deliver notice to the [appointing
12 state official] within 30 days after he loses or misplaces his journal
13 of notarial acts or Official Seal. The fee payable to the [appointing
14 state official] for recording notice of a lost journal or seal is [$2].
15
16   Part IV
17
18 §4-401   Notice and Maximum Fees
19 Every notary public who is not licensed to practice law in this
20 State shall post a notice in his business office, printed in 10 point
21 or larger size type, in the English [and _____] language[s]
22 containing the following statements:
23   (1)_____ [print notary's name], a notary public
24   whose commission expires on _____ [insert
25   expiration date], is not licensed to practice law in this
26   State and may not give legal advice.
27   (2) The maximum fee in this State for notarization of each
28   signature and the proper recordation thereof in the journal
29   of notarial acts is [$2] for each signature notarized.
30   (3) The maximum fee in this State for certification of a
31   facsimile of a document, retaining a facsimile in the
32   notary's file, and the proper recordation thereof in the
33   journal of notarial acts is [$2] for each 8½" x 11" page

retained in the notary's file.

(4) The maximum fee in this State is [insert amount] for any other notarial act performed.

(5) A notary public who charges more than the maximum fees specified, or fails to post this notice, is guilty of official misconduct.

Part V

§4-501   Death

If a notary public dies during the term of his appointment, his heirs or personal representative, as soon as reasonably possible after the notary's death, shall send by certified mail or deliver to the [appointing state official] the deceased notary's journal of notarial acts and all other papers and copies relating to his notarial acts. His heirs or personal representative shall destroy forthwith his official seal.

§4-502   Resignation or Removal

If a notary public no longer desires to be a notary public or has ceased to have a business or residence address in this State, he shall send forthwith by certified mail or deliver to the [appointing state official] a letter of resignation, his journal of notarial acts, and all other papers and copies relating to his notarial acts. He shall destroy forthwith his official seal. His commission shall thereupon cease to be in effect.

§4-503   Revocation of Commission

Immediately after receiving notice from the [appointing state official] that his commission has been revoked, the person whose commission is revoked shall forthwith send by certified mail or deliver to the [appointing state official] his journal of notarial acts and all other papers and copies relating to his notarial acts. He shall destroy forthwith his official seal.

§4-504   Failure to be Reappointed

1 A notary public who is not reappointed to act as a notary public
2 within thirty days after the expiration of his commission shall
3 send forthwith by certified mail or deliver to the [appointing state
4 official] his journal of notarial acts and all other papers and copies
5 relating to his notarial acts. He shall destroy forthwith his official
6 seal.

7 § 4-505   Reappointment
8   (a) No person may be automatically reappointed as a notary
9   public.
10   (b) Every notary public who is an applicant for reappointment
11   as a notary public shall recomply with the provisions of
12   Article II.
13
14
15
16
17
18
19
20
21
22
23
24
25
26
27
28
29
30
31
32
33

Commentary — Article V

The forms prescribed must be substantially followed for the notarization to be recognized and effective in the adopting state. The form in §5-101(6) is not exclusive when executed by a notary not commissioned by this Act, but is exemplary, showing a form that, when used by a person outside of the adopting state, is assured to be understood as a notarization. The adopting state cannot, of course, prescribe notarization procedures to be followed by a notarial officer acting in his official capacity and pursuant to an Act of Congress, nor can it deny effect to such a notarization. A U.S. Consul, U.S. military officer, or foreign notary using the form prescribed in §5-101(6) should include both his title and the authority or law under which he is acting as a notary.

The form of the acknowledgment is prescribed in this Act to emphasize the importance of the statement that is signed by the notary public. If the document is important enough to be notarized, the notary public should be obliged to sign a proper certificate of acknowledgment- that includes the words "known to me to be the person." This clause states that the notary public had sufficient evidence *that the person described in and who executed the document was the person who appeared before him. Further, each §5-101 form states that the document being notarized has been signed for "purposes therein stated," implying competency of the person signing the document and helping to clarify the meaning of the word "acknowledgment." If a person appears to be incompetent, the notary public must use good judgment in determining whether he should perform his notarial act.*

The Executing Witness Form in §5-103 provides for an acknowledgment by a person who is unable to appear before a notary. This form prevents undue hardship caused by illness or inability to obtain a notary.

Section 5-104 prescribes a particular form and procedure for certified copies that is required today because of the invention of machine copiers and also because recorders of public documents now perform such duties. The form for the certification of a facsimile (see § 5-104(c)) of a document makes it clear that the notary must retain a facsimile of the certified facsimile.

Article V
Part I

§ 5-101   Acknowledgment Forms

Certificates of acknowledgment shall be substantially in the following form:

    (1) By an Individual.

        State of _____ , County (and/or City) of _____

        _____. On this _____ day of _____ in the

        year_____ , before me, _____ [name of notary] ,

        a Notary Public in and for said state, personally appeared

        _____ [name of individual] , known to me to be

        the person who executed the within_____ [type

        of document] and acknowledged to me that_____

        _____ [he] executed the same for the purposes therein

        stated.

        _____ [official signature and official seal of

        notary.]

    (2) By a Partner.

        State of _____ , County (and/or City) of _____

        _____ . On this _____ day of _____ in the

        year_____ , before me, _____ [name of notary] ,

        a Notary Public in and for said state, personally appeared

        _____ [name of partner] of _____

        [name of partnership] , known to me to be the person who

        executed the within_____ [type of document]

1   in behalf of said partnership and acknowledged to me that

2   he executed the same for the purposes therein stated.

3   _____ [official signature and official seal of

4   notary.]

5   (3) By a Corporate Officer.

6   State of _____ , County (and/or City) of _____

7   _____. On this _____ day of _____ in the

8   year_____ , before me, _____ [name of notary],

9   a Notary Public in and for said state; personally appeared

10   _____ [name of officer], _____ [title

11   of person (president, vice president, etc.)], _____

12   [name of corporation], known to me to be the person

13   who executed the within _____ [type of

14   document] in behalf of said corporation and acknowl-

15   edged to me that he executed the same for the purposes

16   therein stated.

17   _____ [official signature and official seal of

18   notary.]

19   (4) By an Attorney in Fact for Principal or Surety.

20   State of _____ , County (and/or City) of_____

21   _____. On this_____ day of_____ ,   in the year

22   _____ before me_____ [name of notary], a

23   Notary Public in and for said state, personally appeared

24   _____ [name of attorney in fact], Attorney in

25   Fact for_____ [name of principal or surety],

26   known to me to be the person who executed the within

27   _____ [type of document in behalf of said

28   principal (or surety)], and acknowledged to me that he

29   executed the same for the purposes therein stated.

30   _____ [official signature and official seal of

31   notary.]

32   (5) By a Public Officer, Deputy, Trustee, Administrator,

33   Guardian or Executor.

State of_____, County (and/or City) of_____
_____ . On this _____ day of_____ , in the year
_____, before me _____ [name of notary], a
Notary Public in and for said state, personally appeared
_____[name of person],_____ ,
[person's official title] known to me to be the person who
executed the within_____ [type of document]
in behalf of said_____[public corporation,
agency, political subdivision or estate] and acknowledged
to me that he executed the same for the purposes therein
stated.
_____ [official signature and official seal of
notary.]

(6) By a United States Citizen Who is Outside of the United
States.
_____ [description or location of place where
acknowledgment is taken]
On this_____ day of_____ , in the year_____ ,
before me_____ [name and title of person
acting as a notary and refer to law or authority granting
power to act as a notary], personally appeared _____
_____ , [name of citizen] known to me to be the person
who executed the within_____ [type of
document] and acknowledged to me that _____
[he] executed the same for the purposes therein stated.
_____ [official signature and official seal of
person acting as a notary and refer to law or authority
granting power to act as a notary].

(7) By An Individual Who Cannot Write his Name.
State of_____, County (and/or City) of_____
_____. On this_____ day of_____ , in the year
_____ , before me_____[name of notary], a
Notary Public in and for said state, personally appeared

1   _____ [name of individual], known to me to be

2   the person who, being unable to write his name, made his

3   mark in my presence. I signed his name at his request and

4   in his presence on the within _____ [type of

5   document] and he acknowledged to me and the two

6   witnesses who have signed and printed their names and

7   addresses hereto, that he made his mark on the same for

8   the purposes therein stated.

9   _____ [official signature and official seal of

10   notary.]_____

11   _____ [signatures of two wit-

12   nesses and their addresses.]

13   § 5-102   Affirmation: Procedure, Form

14   (a) If the affirmation to be administered by the notary public

15   is in writing and the person who took the affirmation has

16   signed his name thereto, the notary public shall write or

17   print under the text of the affirmation the following:

18   "Subscribed and affirmed before me this _____ day of ___

19   _____ , 19__."

20   _____ [official signature and official seal of

21   notary.]

22   (b) If the affirmation to be administered by the notary public

23   is not in writing, the notary public shall address the

24   affirmant substantially as follows:

25   "You do solemnly affirm, under the penalty of perjury,

26   that the testimony you shall give in the matter in issue,

27   pending between _____ and _____ ,

28   shall be the truth, the whole truth, and nothing but the

29   truth."

30   § 5-103   Executing Witness Form

31   (a) "Executing witness" as used in this section means an

32   individual who acts in the place of a notary

33   (b) An executing witness may not be related by blood or

1   marriage or have a disqualifying interest as defined in
2   Section 3-102.
3   (c) The affidavit of executing witness for acknowledgment by
4   an individual who does not appear before a notary shall be
5   substantially in the following form:
6   I,_____ [name of executing witness], do
7   solemnly affirm under the penalty of perjury, that _____
8   _____ [name of person who does not appear before a
9   notary], personally known to me, has executed the within
10   _____[type of document] in my
11   presence, and has acknowledged to me that_____
12   [he] executed the same for the purposes therein stated
13   and requested that I sign my name on the within
14   document as an executing witness.
15   _____ [signature of executing witness.]
16   Subscribed and affirmed before me this_____day of___
17   _____19__.
18   _____ [official signature and official seal of
19   notary.]
20 §5-104   Certified Facsimiles of Documents: Procedure, Form
21   (a) A notary public may certify a facsimile of a document if
22   he receives a signed written request stating that:
23   (1) a certified copy or facsimile of the document cannot
24   be obtained from the office of any recorder of public
25   documents or custodian of documents in this State;
26   and,
27   (2) the production of a facsimile, preparation of a copy, or
28   certification of a copy of the document does not
29   violate any state or federal law.
30   (b) Every notary public shall retain a facsimile of each
31   document he has certified as a facsimile of another
32   document, together with other papers or copies relating to
33   his notarial acts.

1   (c) The certification of a facsimile shall be substantially in the

2   following form:

3   State of _____ , County (and/or City) of _____

4   _____ . I, _____ [name of notary], a Notary

5   Public in and for said state, do certify that on _____

6   _____ [date] I carefully compared the attached facsimile of

7   _____ [type of document] and the facsimile I

8   now hold in my possession. They are complete, full, true

9   and exact facsimiles of the document they purport to

10   reproduce.

11   _____ [official signature and official seal of

12   notary.]

13

14

15

16

17

18

19

20

21

22

23

24

25

26

27

28

29

30

31

32

33

Commentary — Article VI

A notary public who exercises a power (Article III) that he has not been authorized to perform is guilty of official misconduct. A notary public who fails to perform the duties prescribed in Article IV is also guilty of official misconduct.

Section 6-102 is necessary to avoid the claims that arise because the employer of a notary has allowed or required his employee-notary to perform notarial acts in violation of the law. There have been instances where the notary was told either to notarize the forgery or be fired.

Fines and imprisonment are optional in certain sections of Article VI, Part II. There are many cases where imprisonment is not necessary because the notary public is bonded and the offense is not serious enough to require incarceration. There are, however, cases of premeditated and intentional fraud or forgery for which the penalty of imprisonment might serve as a deterrent.

Article VI
Part I

§6-101   Liability of Notary and Sureties

A notary public and the surety or sureties on his bond are liable to the persons involved for all damages proximately caused by the notary's official misconduct.

§6-102   Liability of Employer of Notary

The employer of a notary public is also liable to the persons involved for all damages proximately caused by the notary's official misconduct, if:

    (a) the notary public was acting within the scope of his employment at the time he engaged in the official misconduct; and

    (b) the employer consented to the notary public's official

1   misconduct.

2   §6-103   Proximate Cause

3   It is not essential to a recovery of damages that a notary's official
4   misconduct be the only proximate cause of the damages.

5

6   **Part II**

7

8   §6-201   Official Misconduct Defined

9   The term "official misconduct" means the wrongful exercise of a
10   power or the wrongful performance of a duty. The term
11   "wrongful" as used in the definition of official misconduct means
12   unauthorized, unlawful, abusive, negligent, reckless, or injurious.

13   §6-202   Official Misconduct

14   (a) A notary public who knowingly and willfully commits any
15   official misconduct is guilty of a [class of offense] and
16   punishable upon conviction by a fine not exceeding
17   [$5,000] or by imprisonment for not more than [one
18   year], or both.

19   (b) A notary public who recklessly or negligently commits any
20   official misconduct is guilty of a [class of offense] and
21   punishable upon conviction by a fine not exceeding
22   [$1,000].

23   §6-203   Willful Impersonation

24   Any person who acts as, or otherwise willfully impersonates, a
25   notary public while not lawfully appointed and commissioned to
26   perform notarial acts is guilty of a [class of offense] and
27   punishable upon conviction by a fine not exceeding [$5,000] or
28   by imprisonment for not more than [one year], or both.

29   §6-204   Wrongful Possession

30   Any person who unlawfully possesses a notary's journal, official
31   seal or any papers or copies relating to notarial acts, is guilty of a
32   [class of offense] and punishable upon conviction by a fine not
33   exceeding [$1,000].

Commentary — Article VII

The revocation provisions are not mandatory. The state appointing official is vested with discretion, within the bounds of reason and fairness, to uphold the integrity of the Act and of the office of notary public by invoking the revocation sanction in appropriate circumstances. Repeated disregard of the Act's procedural requirements, or conviction of criminal acts calling personal integrity into question, would be serious enough to warrant revocation of a commission. Minor variances with requirements or the belated submission of matter relevant to an application for appointment may not necessitate removal.

The notary must retain his qualification to vote in a state election and maintain a residence or business office within the state, or his commission may be revoked. These requirements are intended to avoid the possibility that a notary, in jail or convicted of a crime that involves loss of voting privilege, could not be removed from office.

Revocation of Commission, Section 7-101 was changed by amendment of January, 1976. Paragraph 5 was added to further clarify the notary's responsibility to be impartial and unbiased. A notary should not use his title of notary public when signing his name to an endorsement of a product, service or person. The title of notary public should not be used to imply that a product is of good quality because the person who signed the endorsement was a notary public. Paragraph 6 was added because some notaries public advertise themselves as notaries public in a language other than English. In some foreign countries the title of notary public can be used only by those who have had many years of education and training. An entirely different problem arises when the notary's employer advertises "Free notary service to customers only." This practice is discriminatory. The notary's employer has also been known to use a valid notarization in advertising intended

1   *to make the buyer believe the offer is more valuable by virtue of*
2   *the display of the notarization or a notary's seal.*
3   *Part II of this Article provides a means of enforcing the ban on*
4   *the unauthorized practice of law. Some notaries public who are*
5   *not attorneys believe that, by virtue of their notarial appoint-*
6   *ments, they are allowed to give legal advice or practice law. The*
7   *practice of law and the practice of a notary public, heretofore,*
8   *have been so entwined and confused that it seems appropriate to*
9   *make this procedure available when the appointing state official*
10   *does not act under the revocation provisions in Part I.*
11
12   **Article VII**
13   **Part I**
14
15   § 7-101   Revocation of Commission
16   The [appointing state official] may revoke the commission of any
17   notary public who during the current term of appointment:
18   (1) submits an application for commission and appointment as
19   a notary public which contains substantial and material
20   misstatement or omission of fact;
21   (2) is convicted of any felony or official misconduct under
22   this Act;
23   (3) fails to exercise the powers or perform the duties of a
24   notary public in accordance with this Act;
25   (4) is adjudged liable or agrees in a settlement to pay damages
26   in any suit grounded in fraud, misrepresentation, imper-
27   sonation, or violation of the state regulatory laws of this
28   State, if his liability is not solely by virtue of his agency or
29   employment relationship with another who engaged in the
30   act for which the suit was brought;
31   *(5) represents or implies from unauthorized use of his title of
32   notary public that he has qualifications, powers, duties,
33   rights, or privileges that by law he does not possess;

*Revision January 1976

1   *(6) allows or permits his name or his title of notary public to
2   be used deceptively, fraudulently, or in false or mislead-
3   ing advertising;
4   (7) engages in the unauthorized practice of law;
5   (8) ceases to be a citizen of the United States or a national of
6   a country which permits American citizens to become
7   notaries public therein;
8   (9) ceases to be a qualified elector of a state;
9   (10) ceases to have a business or residence address in this
10   State; or
11   (11) becomes incapable of reading and writing the English
12   language.
13   A notary's commission may be revoked under the provisions of
14   this Article only if action is taken subject to the rights of the
15   notary public to notice, hearing, adjudication, and appeal.
16
17   **Part II**
18
19   § 7-201   Action for Injunction, Unauthorized Practice of Law
20   Upon his own information or upon complaint of any person, the
21   [attorney general], or his designee, may maintain an action for
22   injunctive relief in [insert name of proper court or courts] against
23   any notary public who renders, offers to render, or holds himself
24   out as rendering any service constituting the unauthorized practice
25   of the law. Any organized bar association in this State may
26   intervene in the action, at any stage of the proceeding, for good
27   cause shown. The action may also be maintained by an organized
28   bar association in this State.
29   § 7-202   Remedies Additional to Those Now Existing
30   The remedies provided in Article VII, Part II are in addition to,
31   and not in substitution for, other available remedies.
32
33

*Revision January 1976

Commentary — Article VIII

The certificate of authority, used to verify the authority of a notary to perform a given act, is provided in this Article primarily to meet the demands for such verification that come from foreign countries. Even if the notarization is to be used in the state where the notary is commissioned, there might be reason to question the authority of the notary to act if the notarization is not complete.

Article VIII

Part I

§8-101   Certificate of Authority

Upon the receipt of a written request, the notarized document and a fee of [$2] payable to the [appointing state official or official of the local office designated by the appointing state official], the office of the [appointing state official or designated local or district office] shall provide a certificate of authority in substantially the following form:

I_____ [appointing state official, or local or district office designated by appointing state official, name and title] of the State of [name of State] which office is an office of record having a seal, certify that _____ [notary's name], by whom the foregoing or annexed document was notarized, was, at the time of the notarization of the same, a Notary Public authorized by the laws of this State to act in this State and to notarize the within _____

_____ [type of document], and I further certify that the Notary's signature on the document is genuine to the best of my knowledge, information, and belief and that such notarization was executed in accordance with the laws of this State.

In testimony whereof, I have affixed my signature and the seal of this office this_____day of_____ 19___ .

_____ [certifying officer's signature, title, jurisdiction, address and the seal affixed near the signature.]

Appendix B
Rules of Notarial Practice

RULES OF NOTARIAL PRACTICE

NOTARIAN ™

Mandate

To competently and impartially
perform all notarizations so that the public-at-
large can rely upon the authenticity of the document
and the identity of the signers.

Rules of Ethics

A NOTARIAN™ should ...

I Avoid being associated with a notarized document
that is likely to be used for false, misleading or
fraudulent purposes.

II Exercise reasonable care to avoid using or allowing
use of the titles of Notary Public and NOTARIAN™
for false, misleading, fraudulent, or discriminatory
purposes.

III Receive a fee for services as a Notary Public-impartial witness and not serve both in the capacity of
Notary Public-impartial witness and advocate-
advisor in connection with the same transaction.

IV Serve as an unbiased and impartial witness and not
give advice regarding the legal sufficiency or subject matter of the document to be notarized.

V Observe the constituent to see that he or she appears to be mentally competent and aware of the
significance and importance of the agreement,

promise or declaration to be notarized.

VI Strive at all times to maintain and preserve the dignity, solemnity and sincerity required in connection with the performance of the notarial act.

Rules of Procedure

A NOTARIAN™ should ...

I Ask the constituent to present proper and sufficient evidence of his or her identity at the time of performance of the notarial act.

II Obtain the signature of the constituent in the journal of notarial acts at the time of performance of the notarial act.

III Compare the signatures made by the constituent on the document and in the journal of notarial acts at the time of performance of the notarial act, with the signatures on the constituent's evidence of identity.

IV Make identifying marks and emboss each page of the document and notary's certificate.

V Record, in the journal of notarial acts, a description of the constituent's evidence of identity, pertinent information about the constituent, and the date, time and place where act was performed, at the time of performance of the notarial act.

VI Record, in the journal of notarial acts, a description of the notarized document and the identifying marks and embossments made on the document and notary's certificate.

VII Keep a copy of a document, for which a certified copy has been made, in a safe place.

VIII Keep the Notary seal, journal of notarial acts, and blank notarial certificates in a locked drawer or compartment.

IX Keep the notary seal, journal of notarial acts, and notary tape in a locked drawer or compartment.

Appendix C

Associations Whose Members Are Often Notaries Public

ASSOCIATIONS WHOSE MEMBERS ARE OFTEN NOTARIES PUBLIC

American Bankers Association
1120 Connecticut Avenue, N.W.
Washington DC 20036

American Bar Association
1155 E. 60th St.
Chicago IL 60637

American Escrow Association
6777 Hollywood Blvd, #605
Los Angeles CA 90028

American Institute of Certified
   Public Accountants
1211 Avenue of the Americas
New York NY 10036

American Insurance Association
   (Insurance Companies)
85 John St.
New York NY 10038

American Land Title
   Association
1828 "L" Street, N.W.
Washington DC 20036

American Paralegal Association
P.O. Box 35233
Los Angeles CA 90035

Independent Insurance
   Agents of America
85 John St.
New York NY 10038

National Association of
   Accountants
919 3rd Ave.
New York NY 10022

National Association of
   Insurance Brokers
111 John Street #2700
New York NY 10038

National Association of
   Legal Secretaries
3005 E. Skelly Dr.
Tulsa OK 74105

National Association of
   Realtors
155 E. Superior St.
Chicago IL 60611

National Association of
   Securities Dealers
1735 "K" St., N.W.
Washington DC 20006

National Notary Association
23012 Ventura Blvd.
Woodland Hills CA 91364
(213) 347-2035

National Savings &
   Loan League
1101 15th Street, N.W.
Washington DC 20005

National Secretaries
   Association
2440 Pershing Road, #G-10
Kansas City MO 64108

National Shorthand
   Reporters
   Association
118 Park St., S.E.
Vienna, VA 22180

National Society of Public
   Accountants
1717 Pennsylvania
   Avenue, N.W.
Washington DC 20006

World Council of Credit Unions
1617 Sherman Avenue
Madison WI 53701

Appendix D

Officers in Each State Who Appoint Notaries Public

TITLE AND ADDRESS OF OFFICERS WHO APPOINT
NOTARIES PUBLIC

Alabama
Secretary of State
Montgomery, AL 36104

Alaska
Lieutenant Governor
Notary Bonds &
  Trademarks Office
Pouch AA
Juneau, AK 99811

Arizona
Secretary of State
1700 West
  Washington St. #702
Phoenix, AZ 85007

Arkansas
Secretary of State
State Capitol
Little Rock, AR 72201

California
Secretary of State
P.O. Box 2071
Sacramento, CA 95810

Colorado
Secretary of State
1575 Sherman St. #211
Denver, CO 80203

Connecticut
Secretary of State
30 Trinity St.
Hartford, CT 06115

Delaware
Secretary of State
Townsend Building
Dover, DE 19901

District of Columbia
The Secretariat
District Building #101
14th and E St. NW
Washington, D.C. 20004

Florida
Secretary of State
Department of State
Capitol Building
Tallahassee, FL 32304

Georgia
Secretary of State
214 State Capitol
Atlanta, GA 30334

Hawaii
Attorney General
State Capitol Building
415 S. Beretania St.
Honolulu, HI 96813

Idaho
Secretary of State
Boise, ID 83770

Illinois
Secretary of State
Capitol Building #109
Springfield, IL 62756

Indiana
Secretary of State
201 State House
Indianapolis, IN 46204

Iowa
Secretary of State
Capitol Building
Des Moines, IA 50319

Kansas
Secretary of State
State House, 2nd Fl.
Topeka, KS 66612

Kentucky
Secretary of State
State Capitol #153
Frankfort, KY 40601

Louisiana
Secretary of State
State Capitol
Baton Rouge, LA 70804

Maine
Secretary of State
Corporation and
    UCC Division
State Office Building
Augusta, ME 03444

Maryland
Secretary of State
State House
Annapolis, MD 21404

Massachusetts
Governor
Executive Council
State House #184
Boston, MA 02133

Michigan
Governor
Department of State
Great Seal and Trademark
    Section
Capitol Building #114
Lansing, MI 48918

Minnesota
Governor
Department of Commerce
Metro Square Building,
    5th Fl.
St. Paul, MN 55101

Mississippi
Secretary of State
P.O. Box 136
Jackson, MS 39205

Missouri
Secretary of State
P.O. Box 788
Jefferson City, MO 65101

Montana
Governor
State Capitol
Helena, MT 59601

Nebraska
Secretary of State
State Capitol
Lincoln, NB 68509

Nevada
Secretary of State
State Capitol Building
Carson City, NV 89710

New Hampshire
Secretary of State

State House
Concord, NH 03301

New Jersey
Secretary of State
State House #101
Trenton, NJ 08625

New Mexico
Secretary of State
Legislative-Executive Bldg.
  #400
Santa Fe, NM 87503

New York
Secretary of State
Department of State
162 Washington Ave.
Albany, NY 12231

North Carolina
Secretary of State
116 West Jones St.
101 Administration Bldg.
Raleigh, NC 27603

North Dakota
Secretary of State
Capitol Bldg.
Bismark, ND 58501

Ohio
Governor
State House
Columbus, OH 43215

Oklahoma
Secretary of State
101 State Capitol Bldg.
Oklahoma City, OK 73105

Oregon
Secretary of State
State Capitol Bldg. #141

Salem, OR 97310

Pennsylvania
Secretary of
  The Commonwealth
Department of State
North Office Bldg. #305
Harrisburg, PA 17120

Rhode Island
Secretary of State
State House #219
Providence, RI 02903

South Carolina
Governor
Department of State
P.O. Box 11350
Columbia, SC 29211

South Dakota
Secretary of State
Department of State
Pierre, SD 57501

Tennessee
Secretary of State
C1-101 Central Service Bldg.
Nashville, TN 37219

Texas
Secretary of State
State Capitol
Austin, TX 78711

Utah
Secretary of State
203 State Capitol Bldg.
Salt Lake City, UT 84114

Vermont
Secretary of State
State House
Montpelier, VT 05602

Virginia

Secretary of Commonwealth
Ninth Street Office Building
Richmond, VA 23219

Washington

Governor
Division of Professional
  Licensing
P.O. Box 649
Olympia, WA 98504

West Virginia

Secretary of State
Capitol Building
Charleston, WV 25305

Wisconsin

Secretary of State
112 West, State Capitol
Madison, WI 53702

Wyoming

Secretary of State
Capitol Bldg.
Cheyenne, WY 82002

Appendix E
National Notary Census

NATIONAL NOTARY CENSUS

State	No. Of Notaries 1972	No. Of Notaries 1977	Total State Population (1970 Census)	No. Of Notaries Per Thousand Population (1977)
ALABAMA	N/A	61,978	3,444,165	18
ALASKA	4,500	7,626	302,173	25
ARIZONA	35,000	75,000	1,772,482	42
ARKANSAS	20,000	30,000	1,923,295	16
CALIFORNIA	120,000	123,000	19,953,134	6
COLORADO	30,000	43,000	2,207,259	20
CONNECTICUT	24,000	29,000	3,032,217	9
DELAWARE	2,275	3,250	548,104	6
DISTRICT OF COLUMBIA	2,700	2,800	756,510	4
FLORIDA	120,000	170,000	6,789,443	25
GEORGIA	70,000	95,000	4,589,575	21
HAWAII	1,500	1,550	769,913	2
IDAHO	8,500	10,000	713,008	14
ILLINOIS	150,000	160,000	11,113,976	14
INDIANA	50,600	60,000	5,193,669	11
IOWA	28,000	30,012	2,825,041	11
KANSAS	27,500	75,000	2,249,071	33
KENTUCKY	20,000	48,000	3,219,311	15
LOUISIANA	8,000	10,000	3,643,180	3
MAINE	9,800	9,500	993,663	10
MARYLAND	40,000	75,000	3,922,399	19
MASSACHUSETTS	75,000	110,000	5,689,170	19
MICHIGAN	95,000	130,000	8,875,083	15
MINNESOTA	42,000	64,000	3,805,069	17
MISSISSIPPI	10,500	35,000	2,216,912	16
MISSOURI	10,000	72,000	4,677,399	15
MONTANA	6,900	10,000	694,409	14
NEBRASKA	16,000	16,000	1,483,791	11
NEVADA	4,653	7,853	488,738	2
NEW HAMPSHIRE	10,000	13,000	737,681	17
NEW JERSEY	125,000	94,000	7,168,164	13
NEW MEXICO	11,500	17,000	1,016,000	17
NEW YORK	141,223	160,000	18,241,266	9
NORTH CAROLINA	40,000	42,000	5,082,059	8
NORTH DAKOTA	7,000	7,900	617,761	13
OHIO	N/A	91,000	10,652,017	9
OKLAHOMA	14,000	31,500	2,559,253	12
OREGON	20,000	24,500	2,091,385	12
PENNSYLVANIA	40,000	55,000	11,793,909	5
RHODE ISLAND	8,500	10,000	949,723	11
SOUTH CAROLINA	37,399	60,982	2,590,516	24
SOUTH DAKOTA	10,240	9,675	666,257	15
TENNESSEE	35,000	50,000	3,924,164	13
TEXAS	179,000	240,000	11,196,730	21
UTAH	14,000	22,000	1,059,273	21
VERMONT	2,500	4,700	444,732	11
VIRGINIA	45,000	45,000	4,648,494	10
WASHINGTON	27,000	32,000	3,409,169	9
WEST VIRGINIA	N/A	9,600	1,744,237	5
WISCONSIN	30,000	50,000	4,417,933	11
WYOMING	4,211	6,800	332,416	20

Appendix F

Sample Forms for Certificates of Acknowledgment and Certified Copy

These forms are presented as examples. If the form is not prescribed by law, changes may be necessary that should be made under the direction of an attorney.

1. **Certificate of acknowledgment on oath of a subscribing (credible) witness. Acknowledgment by a person who does not appear before the Notary.**

I, _____ (name of subscribing witness), do solemnly swear (or affirm) that _____ (name of person who does not appear before the Notary), personally known to me, has executed the within _____ (type of document) in my presence, and has acknowledged to me that _____ (he) executed the same for the purposes therein stated and requested that I sign my name on the within document as a subscribing witness.
_____ (signature of subscribing witness)
Subscribed and sworn (or affirmed) before me this _____ day of _____ 19 _____.
_____ (official signature and official seal of Notary)

2. **Certificate of acknowledgment on oath of a subscribing (credible) witness. Acknowledgment by a person whose identity is proven to the Notary.**

I, _____ (name of subscribing witness), do solemnly swear (or affirm) that _____ (name and address of person whose identity is proven), personally known to me, has executed the within _____ (type of document) in my presence, and has acknowledged to me that _____ (he) executed the same for the purposes therein stated and requested that I sign my name on the within document as a subscribing witness.
_____ (signature of subscribing witness)
Subscribed and sworn (or affirmed) before me this _____ day of _____ 19 _____.
_____ (official signature and official seal of Notary)

State of _____ County of _____
On this _____,_____ day of _____ 19 _____, before me, _____
(name of Notary), a Notary Public in and for said state, personally
appeared _____, (name and address of person whose identity is proven by subscribing witness) whose identity has been
proven to me under the oath (or affirmation) of _____
(name of subscribing witness), and acknowledged to me that
_____ he) executed the same for the purposes therein
stated. Witness my hand and official seal.
_____ (official signature and official seal of Notary)

3. Certificate of acknowledgment for a person who is unable to write. Signature by Mark (X).

State of _____, County (and/or City) of _____.
On this _____ day of _____ 19 _____, before me
_____ (name of Notary), a Notary Public in and for said
state, personally appeared _____ (name of person unable
to write), known to me to be the person who, being unable to write
his name, made his mark in my presence. I signed his name at his
request and in his presence on the within _____ (type of
document) and he acknowledged to me and the two witnesses who
have signed and printed their names and addresses hereto, that he
made his mark on the same for the purposes therein stated. Witness
my hand and official seal.
_____ (official signature and official seal of Notary)
_____ (signatures of two witnesses and their addresses)

4. Certificate for a certified copy of an original or facsimile.

State of _____, County (and/or City) of _____. I,
_____ (name of Notary), a Notary Public in and for said
state, do certify that on _____ (date) I carefully compared
the attached facsimile of _____ (type of document) and the
facsimile I now hold in my possession. They are complete, full, true
and exact facsimiles of the document they purport to reproduce. Witness my hand and official seal.
_____ (official signature and official seal of Notary)

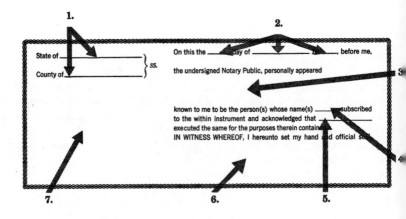

1.

2.

State of _____
County of _____ } ss.

On this the _____ day of _____, before me,

the undersigned Notary Public, personally appeared

3.

known to me to be the person(s) whose name(s) _____ subscribed
to the within instrument and acknowledged that _____
executed the same for the purposes therein contained.
IN WITNESS WHEREOF, I hereunto set my hand and official seal.

4.

7.   **6.**   **5.**

FILLING OUT A
CERTIFICATE OF ACKNOWLEDGMENT

1. "State" and "County" in which the Notary is performing his Notarial Act.
2. Actual day, month and year that the party (or parties) appeared before the Notary and acknowledged that he, she or they signed the document.
3. Name(s) of the party or parties actually appearing before the Notary who have signed the document. Initials and spelling of all names should be identical on the acknowledgment form, in the signature on the document, and in the body of the document itself. A line should be drawn through any blanks in this area to prevent additional names being inserted after the document and attached acknowledgment form have left the Notary's office.
4. "Are" or "is" depending on the number of party (or parties), whose name(s) are in the blank under #3.
5. "He," "she," or "they" depending on the sex of the individual and number of party (or parties).
6. Signature of the Notary, followed by his title (Notary Public) and any other information required by state law.
7. The Notary's official seal impression as clearly and legibly as possible. The Notary's Rubber Stamp Seal and/or Notary's Seal Embosser should never cover any writing other than the letters "L.S." if the Notary has used a Seal Embosser.

INDEX

Absent parties, 41

Absentee voter's ballot, 21-23
form of affidavit, 22
form of Notary's certificate, 22

Acknowledgments, 9, 15-21, 43
certificate of, 4
defined, 15
form of, 16-20, 49
notarization of, 11
proofs of, 5, 20-21

Address of Notary, 11, 20, 30, 42, 47
on absentee voter's ballot, 22
on acknowledgment, 20
on jurats, 25
on rubber stamps, 20, 30, 34, 35,
42, 47

Affiant, 22, 23, 24

Affidavits, 23-25
for absentee voter's ballot, 22
defined, 23
early use of, 3, 4
notarization of, 11, 23-25

Affirmations. SEE Oaths

Agreements, 9-10, 11, 15, 19
early history of, 1-3

Application for appointment,
Notary's, 53-54

Bills of exchange (inland and foreign)
early use of, 3

Blanks (in a document)
to be filled in, 17, 37, 40

Bond, Notary's. SEE Notary bond

Bonding company, 54-55

Certificate of acknowledgment.
SEE Acknowledgments

Certificate of Authentication, 49

Certificate of authority, 49-50
form of, 49-50

Certificate of Official Character, 49

Certificate of Prothonotary, 49

Certification or certificate.
SEE Notarization

Certified copies, 5, 25-26, 47

Commission expiration, 56
disposition of record books, 42
disposition of seal embosser, 35, 42

Commission expiration date, 11, 30,
42, 47
on absentee voter's ballot, 22
on acknowledgments, 20
on jurats, 25
on rubber stamps, 20, 30, 34, 35,
42, 47

Commissioner of Deeds, 6

Competency, of Notary, 46-47, 53-57
of parties, 21, 48-49

"Conservators of the peace," 56

Constituent, 51

Conveyances, 4

Copies, conforming of, 43

Corrections, 40
initialing of, 37, 40

Custodian of Public
Documents or Records.
SEE Recorder of Public Documents

Date
of acknowledgment, 20
of official act, 36, 37
that parties signed, 36, 37
in record book, 36, 37

Death, of Notary
disposition of record book, 42
disposition of seal embosser, 35, 42

Deeds
acknowledgment of, 4

Depositions, 27
early use of, 3-4
notarization of, 11
taking oaths, 23-24

INDEX (Continued)

Disqualifying interest, 51-52
    advocate, 45-46, 51-52
    beneficial (financial), 51-52

Documents
    notarization of, 11-12, 34-35, 40
    out of state, 49-50
    recording of, 11-12, 26, 31-32

Documents, Recorder of. SEE
    Recorder of Public Documents

Driver's license. SEE Identification
    cards

Embosser, SEE Seal embosser

Errors and Omissions Insurance
    Policy, 39, 56
    SEE Corrections

Fees, Notary's
    most schedules out of date, 38
    to be noted in record book, 36, 38

"Femme couvert," 49

Financial interest, of Notary, 51-52

Foreign-language documents, 46-47

Forgery
    correct use of seal embosser
        prevents, 12, 30-31, 32-34, 35,
        60
    of identification, 17-18, 59-61
    of signatures, 29, 59-60

Identification cards, 17-18
    driver's license, 18
    note kinds of in record book, 19, 37,
        38-39, 43, 61
    passport, 18, 30

Identification of parties, 9, 17-19, 46
    for absentee voter's ballot, 22-23
    on acknowledgment, 17-19
    for jurats, 25

Ignorance, Notary's
    not an excuse, 56

Incompetency
    of Notaries, 46-47, 53-57
    of parties, 21, 48-49

Jurats
    defined, 23
    forms of, 24
    noted in record book, 25, 36, 38

Jurisdiction, of Notaries, 11
    on absentee voter's ballot, 22
    on acknowledgment, 16, 20
    on certificate of authority, 50
    on jurats, 25
    on rubber stamps, 20, 30, 34, 35,
        42, 47

Justices of the peace, 56

Known vs. unknown, 18, 19

Law, illegal practice. SEE practice of
    law

Legal advice (Notary should obtain),
    62
    on corrections, 40
    on form of affidavit, 25
    on judging competence of parties,
        21, 48-49
    in preparing legal documents, 45-46

Legibility of writing, 29, 30, 33-34,
    47-48

Liability, of Notary, 53-57
    to bonding company, 55
    on competence of parties, 48-49
    if financially interested, 51-52
    in identification of parties, 19, 59
    on jurats, 25
    in keeping original documents
    necessity of keeping record book,
        35-36, 39, 61
    if physically disabled, 46
    on proofs of acknowledgment, 21
    to public, 45, 53, 55, 56

Loose certificates, 33-34
    handling of, 40-41
    noted in record book, 37

"L.S.," 4, 25, 32-34, 39, 48
    defined, 32

Maritime protests, 3

INDEX (Continued)

Marriages, 55-56

Mental disability
of Notary, 46
of parties, 21, 48-49

Ministerial, vs. judicial, 2, 3, 9, 53

Minors
competence of, 49
and identification cards, 18

Misconduct, by Notary, 53, 55-56

Mortgages, 4

Name, of Notary, 42, 47
on absentee voter's ballot, 22
on acknowledgment, 16
on certificate of authority, 49, 50
on jurats, 25
on rubber stamp, 20, 30, 34, 35, 42,
47
on seal embosser, 12, 30, 35, 43

Name, of signer,
on acknowledgment and document,
17
noted in record book, 36, 38, 41, 43,
61

Negotiable instruments, 27
early use of, 3

Notarius, 1

Notarization
defined, 11
necessity for, 11-12

Notary bond, 32, 39, 45, 54-55
form of, 54-55

Notary laws
history of, 1-7
on mental and physical competence,
46-49
on out-of-state documents, 49-50
and practice of law, 45-46
on record books, 35-36
regarding negotiable instruments, 27
on schedules of fees, 38

Notary Public
defined, 9
duties of, 9-10
history of, 1-7
summary of practices, 42-43

Notary tape, Adhesive
over critical areas, 61

Oaths, 23-25
for absentee voter's ballot, 21-22
for affidavits, 24-25
defined, 23
early use of, 4-5
forms of, 22, 23
notarization of, 11
for proof of acknowledgment, 20-21

Out-of-state documents, 49-50

Photographic reproduction advances
in machines for, 12, 31-32, 42,
59-62
forging of signature, 18
photocopying identification, 17-18,
60-61
in Recorder's office, 25-26
of seal embosser's indentations, 12,
30-32, 59-60

Physical disability
of Notary, 46-47
of parties, 21, 48-49

Practice of law
acknowledgment forms, 15, 19, 21
judging what constitutes, 21, 25,
45-46
negotiable instruments and
depositions, 27

Proof of acknowledgment. SEE
Acknowledgments

Public Documents, Recorder of. SEE
Recorder of Public Documents

Public Records
entering documents in, 11-12, 26,
31-32

INDEX (Continued)

Record book, of Notary, 10, 35-36, 43
  checklist of entries, 36-42
  early use of, 5
  oaths and affidavits, 25
  to avoid fraud, 19, 32, 38-39, 60, 61
  value of, 35-36, 38-39

Recorder of Public Documents, 47-48
  certified copies, 25-26
  duties of, 47-48
  immediate transmittal of documents
    to, 31-32
  importance of date of document to,
    37

Removal from office, Notary's
  disposition of record book, 42
  disposition of seal embosser, 35, 42

Resignation, of Notary, disposition
  of record book, 42
  disposition of seal embosser, 35, 42

Responsibilities, Notary's, 32, 36,
  45-46, 59-62

Rubber stamp, of Notary, 20, 30,
  34-35, 42, 43, 47

Schedule of fees. SEE Fees

Seal embosser, 5, 11, 12, 30-31,
  47-48
  on acknowledgments, 20
  on certificate of authority, 50
  on certified copies, 25-26
  description of, 30
  disposition of, 35, 42
  on jurats, 25
  on loose certificates, 33-34
  noted in record book, 37, 41
  to avoid forgery, 12, 30-32, 47-48,
    60-61
  where to place, 32-34

Seals, 9-10
  definition of, 1-2
  early use of, 1-2
  private, 1, 2, 4

rubber stamp seal, 20, 30, 34-35,
  42, 43, 47
scrawl or scroll seal, 4-5

Signature (of Notary), 9, 60
  on absentee voter's ballot, 22
  on acknowledgments, 17, 20
  on certificate of authority, 49-50
  on certified copies, 25, 26
  form of, 29-30, 42
  on jurats, 24-25
  legibility of, 29, 30, 47-48
  notarization of own, 52
  on rubber stamp, 42

Signature (of parties), 59-60
  legibility of, 47-48
  by mark, 4, 21
  to be made in record book, 36,
    38-39, 43, 60
  verification of, 18

S.S. (symbol), 16

Telephone, identifying party, 17, 55

Testimonium Clause,
  form of, 20, 29

Title, of Notary, 11, 42, 47
  on absentee voter's ballot, 22
  on acknowledgments, 16, 20
  on certificate of authority, 49
  on jurats, 24-25
  on rubber stamps, 20, 30, 34-35, 42,
    47

Venue, 16

Voluntary acknowledgment,
  defined, 19, 27

Voter's ballot. SEE Absentee voter's
  ballot

Witnesses
  depositions, 3-4
  noted in record book, 37, 41-42
  for proofs of acknowledgment, 5, 20

Women, contracts by, 49